Cry Bullies:

Protecting yourself against social muggers and victimhood aggression.

Written and published by Robert Juliano at Amazon

2018

Amazon Edition License Notes

Dedication: To my very patient wife, Rebecca Hedreen.

Acknowledgements

Very few authors come up with a book on their own. I'm not one of them. I'd like to thank the following people for helping me…

My wife, Rebecca Hedreen, for putting up with me on this trip.
Marc MacYoung, for patient advice and guidance..
Aaron and the semi-saturday card game and philosophical society.

Table of Contents

Pardon him. Theodotus: he is a barbarian,

and thinks that the customs of his tribe

and island are the laws of nature. -- George B. Shaw.

Forward

Pardon Bob Juliano, for he is an academic and a nerd.

In other words, he's not a professional writer or spinmeister. He's not as smooth, polished or artistic in crafting words as a novelist. He's not as glib, rhetorical, persuasive or practiced in manipulation as commentators and pundits. He's not what you're used to.

What he is is someone who knows what he's talking about – especially when it comes to how people will verbally and emotionally attack you.

Cry Bullies: Protecting yourself against social muggings and victimhood aggression is a study in the common attacks, tactics, rhetoric, distractions, tricks and insults that have created such division and hostility in this country.

What many people don't realize is how amazingly predictable these strategies are. Nor do they know how easy they are to defeat them once you know them. And not knowing is pretty painful.

Being attacked this way (and make no mistake, it is an attack) has become both common and is an academic conceit. It's commonly used by people who are pretending to be smarter to you, put you down and shut you up. (They're right. You're wrong. So go sit in the corner and feel ashamed about how wrong you are.)

As it is an academic conceit, it makes sense to go to an academic to learn how to blow it out of the water. So despite the writing style being — not surprisingly — academic now and then it's well worth working through. Not just so you can protect yourself and others against such attacks, but well, let's admit it, it's kind of fun to say, "Torpedoes away!" Marc MacYoung

If a behavior is wrong, it is wrong no matter who is doing it. While many will justify why they are doing it, the ones you really have to watch out for are the ones who are doing it and denying that is exactly what they're doing.
Marc MacYoung

Chapter One: What they are

Ever see happen or been the target of it?

You: "Chicago's crime scene is getting completely out of hand."

SJW: "That's Racist!"

You (confused) : "When did I say anything about Race?"

SJW: "You are being problematic about a very large community of People Of Color!"

You (trying to stay calm) : I was talking about the crime levels and the safety…"

SJW, interrupting: "DO YOU HAVE **ANY** IDEA WHAT YOU SOUND LIKE?

You (feeling attacked) : "Hey! What's going on? I was trying to talk about making things safer…"

SJW: OH! MY! GOD! Can you be ANY more SEXIST? **MANSPLAINING** LIKE THAT!?"

You (wondering what the hell happened): "Why are you yelling about other things?"

Let me lay out some uncomfortable facts:

1.) There's a hell of a lot of messed-up/hurt people out there.
2.) A lot of people are looking to put that hurt on someone else –
   either by attacking you to vent
off internal pressure, or to scare third parties into doing things for
the hurt person.
3.) They need a safe target.
4.) In order to stay "safe" in their attack, they stick with well-run
   reliable patterns.
5.) They get off on it. (Abusing others gives them a sense of
   power and control.)

I wrote this book to serve as a quick and dirty guide to
dealing with certain types of people. People that delight in stirring
the pot and spreading ill will: the social mugger. There are a lot of
names for these kinds of people: wind up merchant, shit pot
stirrer, troublemaker, gadfly, "Special Snowflake," etc. I'm going
to flash my nerd credentials by quoting *Firefly*: "there ain't
nothing worse than a monster who thinks he's right with God."
Their pain and dysfunction aside, a lot of the people playing these
games think they are right with God – and they're coming after

you.

I've crawled through Academia for 30 years. During this time, I've seen the general rise of smugness and the fall of critical thinking. This parallels the trend of shifting from teaching people 'how to think' to 'what to think.' People who have been indoctrinated into this new 'Academic' style sincerely believe that they are educated, knowledgable, and thinking clearly on the subject. They have fallen into dogma. Smugness, rhetoric, hostility, and aggression are used to cover the holes in these beliefs, while pretending to be logical and reasonable. What's scary is how often they are encouraged to go out and proselytize. This isn't rational. These are true believers seeking to convert or punish.

Also, I've spent about the same amount of time in 'normal' and less than normal groups. I've seen this spread of convert or be punished fervor spread from Academia into other circles. This is how it can come into your life even if you are far from your college days. You see it on social media, in conversation, you see it on the news as protesters push for further and further extremes.

A simple way to think of social muggers is seeing them as little traveling rain clouds. Rain clouds travel in predictable lines pushed by wind ,and they piss down on you (and piss you off) wherever they go. Sometimes a number of them will clump together, and create wind, lightning, etc. If they were real rain clouds, you could change course to avoid them, put on a rain coat, grab your umbrella - or you can sit there and get wet. The difference is, real rain clouds don't follow you, or actively insert themselves into your life. This makes not getting wet a little more complicated. You'll need more than just an umbrella. That's what this book is about.

We'll talk more about how they get away with this later. For now, a quick summation is that they rely on other people's good manners (They are turning your good manners against you.) What we are going to covering in this book is how not to get wet, without creating a scene – by revealing how far from logic and critical thinking - and even the facts -they really are. This is about how to shut them down, keep your cool, and not look like the bad guy.

This book shows defenses, counters, and ways to fight back – active counter debating, active call outs of dubious "facts" or "reliable studies," and active support for groups fighting social mugging.

I'm skipping negotiation tactics for two reasons: 1.) Negotiation tactics are covered by a lot of authors. 2.) Negotiation requires two parties willing to actually compromise. Some of these rainclouds stir the pot to advance a cause, some mess with others to try and lessen their own pain, and some are just outright predators. There are people out there using these <reverb> SOCIAL JUSTICE </reverb> tools to score themselves a string of sexual conquests. It isn't cool when the predators use traditional/mainstream covers, and it isn't cool when they use social justice masks. Either way, these predators hide behind masks and roles.

(Before we really kick this off, I have to make a few assumptions for anyone reading this book. I have to assume the people doing the character-mugging are not a boss, not law enforcement, and not pointing weapons at you. That's a whole different ball of wax.)

Language is one of our operating systems. We 'think' in concepts and words. When we work on something, we give it a name. When we talk with people, we give that a name. When we like someone's cooking style, we give *that* a name. That way, we can trade ideas and services as barter with our friends, build trading networks, and create long lasting civilizations. The words someone uses gives you an idea about the actions they think are options. If you listen and watch what someone does, you've got a pretty good idea what they will try to do to you.

When people try to change the meanings of words, they are trying to change the concepts in other people's operating

system. They are trying to hack a group's operating system. It doesn't matter if that's a local node (that would be your own house rules) or the background culture's laws. There was a guy named Antonio Gramsci, who wrote glowingly about "subversive communications" (culture hacking, if you will) and the need for using it to change society. By controlling the background language that people use, you shape the ways people could describe things. Shaping other people's thoughts narrows their mental menu of habits and action. That sounds a lot like soft brainwashing. (Look up Newspeak in your favorite search engine.) One way to fight some of Gramsci's ideas is to look up and learn about "E-Prime" on the web. It was created by a guy named David Bourland (E-Prime, where there "is no is." There is only "appears to be.") Unfortunately, controlling the language is also a trick that predatory people use to slip into a group, when searching for new victims. (Please note that I'm not trying to suggest that all of the rainclouds are predators. I am trying to point out that many rainclouds may have been exposed to predatory behavior. It's a tradition they often keep up.) I give you that tidbit about word games because that's mostly what they play and how they operate – and attack. We'll talk more about this later.That said, there are many traits rainclouds and predators share. A quick list:
>It's all about them

\>Other people matter less

\>They can ignore objections when they try to force other people

\>Words that show threats

\>They get angry quickly

\>Vengeance is their thing

\>They ride emotional roller coasters

\>They're always justified no matter how bad their behavior

\>They need to hide their games behind a noble cause

\>Physical tantrums

1) *It's all about them* – Is the raincloud getting their way more important than other people's welfare? Do their "wants" always seem to override other people's "needs?" The speed that a conversation goes to 'all about me' is a serious red flag – the faster the shift, the bigger the red flag. "This isn't about you" is a favorite phrase spouted by rainclouds. That phrase has a built in assumption that you have-to/will defer to them. It's a form of gas-lighting that is built on the assumption that they are better, and you just need to get with the program. (*Gas-lighting: ways of slowly messing up someone's head, by constantly saying or at least implying that you know someone else's real thoughts better than they do. It's also getting them to doubt what they 'know' or have seen you do. Gas-lighting is used to control other people, or to get sick kicks.*) They think

that the world "owes" them what they want. In order to make sure they get 'paid,' they will try to make you feel bad for not doing what they want – and making you feel bad leads to the next point...

2) *Other people matter less* – Look out for the joker who constantly makes comments to shut down or bring down other people. It can be easy to spot: Look for the put down artist and look for his victim. The person putting down others shows a big problem in most rainclouds: many rainclouds often think they are, or should be, "better" than other people. When you dig deeper into these guys, they can give off a "rightful ruler to the world, unjustly usurped" vibe. Such people often feel they have a right to 'take' what they want. They often hide this by using arguments that meet a host group's approval. ("You are the same skin color as someone that I saw drive into a country club, so I have a right to take your stuff" sounds pretty stupid. How is this statement more or less logical than the more erudite terms about privilege?)

3) From points one and two, we get a third. If your rights/position doesn't matter, and they are better than you, then it's okay for them to show you your place – *and it's okay to ignore the parts where you object.* They will roll through a script and

ignore your polite complaints that you might use to try to extract yourself from the conversation. Worse, if you do dare to stand up to them, they'll both dismiss and condemn. Comments like "you don't really mean that" and "your complaint shows your fragility" and "it isn't about you" are red flags that someone is trying to shut you down/negate you. When a predator uses negation, they are trying to rewrite the other person's thoughts, feelings and needs to match up to what the predator wants – same with the rainclouds. In other words, they are trying to *Gaslight* you. Remember, it's all about them.

4) *Words that show threats*. A person's choice of words shows how they think. (This one can head from nasty social games over to the Saturday night knife and gun club at your local Emergency Room.) There were these two guys named Sapir and Whorf that talked about this one. A super quick version is that a culture has more words to describe what they care about. The classic idea is that the Inuit/Eskimo have something like 47 different words for different types of snow/ice, but no one word for 'all types of snow' or 'all types of ice.' If they keep using the language, the subject is obviously on their minds a lot. Language can show habits. Habits can suggest actions. If accusatory 'yous,' condemnation

and hostility are common in the person's words, watch out.

5) *They get angry quickly.* By itself, being angry doesn't mean much. Adding anger to the rest of this list – or having it as a regular backbeat – can be a big red flag. This is when you have to ask some questions: How fast does this person go from 'normal' to angry? How low is that flashpoint? How often do they get pissed off? How big or little is what they're getting angry over? While we're at it, how well 'rehearsed' is their anger?

6) *Vengeance is their thing...* Once the raincloud has flashed over into the angry zone, how long do they hang onto a grudge? Do they keep a garden of grudges? Do they sulk in a corner and glare from across the room? Do they make a habit of 'getting even' for every real or imagined insult? This can point out an obsessive personality – which can turn into a case of 'have to win.' Often these will be smear campaigns and anonymous harassment. (Google 'doxxing.')

7) *They ride emotional roller coasters.* Most people have a cycle of emotions and moods over time.How fast and wide does that person swing on the cycle? Be careful around people who can go from wildly happy to wired-up anger about something with

the flip of an invisible switch. That kind of mental mis-wiring leads to them feeling they've got a 'right' to wreck havoc and mayhem. Worse, they will say they have the right to break things when their feeling get hurt. When you see someone walking around glowering with anger, quickly flashing into their own red zone, you can expect them to start 'flailing for feelings." There is a difference between a person with manic depressive issues, and a person using these mood swings as a way to control other people. Please don't let predatory people use hurting people as cover.

8) They're always justified no matter how bad their behavior. This goes beyond excuses and moves into self-permission. It's not only a justification for why they have no choice ("I can't help myself because....") It's their shield against criticism over what they're doing. ("I can't be expected to meet those standards because I'm ...") It's also a green light to attack you.

9.) *They need to hide their games behind a noble cause.* These people need to build a scene that shows them as a noble hero, rousing the populace against that which is evil. If they can't look noble, their games can't hide the social mugging.

10.) *Physical tantrums* – Look out for those who break things around them, as a *hobby*. They hit the walls, kick things, just flail away with their hands, etc. Look up "SJW tantrums" or "SJW meltdowns for great examples. Someone jumping into chanting and frenzy punching the air often starts looking for walls and people. It's only a short step from someone using a chair to wreck some property, to taking that chair to wreck *you*.

When you see/hear/have-to-deal-with someone scolding you to change your ways, ask yourself a question: Who benefits? That scolding tone suggests that the raincloud is upset. The usual habit of blaming the raincloud's target suggests the raincloud is trying to get you pissed off enough to pay less attention to thinking things through - one of the easiest times to switch changing meanings is when people are tired, or their emotions are stirred up. (It's easier to stalk prey when the prey doesn't think ahead. Don't be prey.)

How will the raincloud's target benefit from getting yelled at? Most likely, the target won't benefit – the 'suggested' changes only benefit the raincloud, and usually have an "others must convert" vibe. Not a cool thing to do.This is a long, winding way to show the levels of a "simple" difference in suggested language change. For instance: "Straight" versus "Cis-het." Both describe being attracted to the opposite sex – but the second term isn't standard English. Making a request that others call your by your favorite new pronoun is a request – and suggests that the speaker shows polite manners. *Demanding* that others refer to you and others by that new pronoun suggests that the speaker has power or superior status over the listener/target. Demanding that other people change their own pronouns suggests that the "change agent" has *dominance* over other's choices.

How they got that way

"

Oh just so you know. The term "Social Justice Warrior" (SJW) splashed onto the net around 2009, when socialist Will Shetterly published his "Do Not Engage" article. *The Making of a Social Justice Warrior* has Shetterly following the SJW's at least as far back as 2005. (For irony, think about the fact that an actual socialist was yelling at people claiming to fight for social justice.) There is an urban myth going around Liberal/Leftist/Hipster circles where "the rightwing nut-jobs" created the term to smear people and "demonize" those Leftist circles. In fact, those Leftist circles created that term for "empowerment" - a person isn't just a scold against hurtful speech. Instead, they are a 'Social Justice Warrior,' bravely fighting against violent speech. Shetterly's story shows a different story, with SJW focused crowds promoting intimidation, attempts at censorship, virtue signaling, and mob tactics.

Let's talk about logic and rhetoric for a bit. Logic is a mode of reasoning that uses testable statements and observations, to apply those observations to the real world. "A Squared plus B squared equals C squared" is always true. Every carpenter uses this form of basic logic when working. "A person can not be in two places at the same time" is always true. This is used in court rooms. Rhetoric is the study and use of effectively speaking and writing to persuade people. The speech or writing doesn't have to be sincerely held beliefs, nor does it have to be true. It merely has to convince others. Rhetoric appeals to *Ethos* (What is socially accepted in a community) and *Pathos* (strong emotion.) A quick version is: Logical arguments want to test their facts, test their own logical links, and test their assumptions. Rhetorical arguments boil down to "forget your facts. Forget your reasoning. What about my *feelings*?"

I tell you this so you understand Rainclouds aren't just about their feeling. They have some battle tested attack strategies and tricks up their sleeves.

Man's enemies are not demons, but human beings like himself.
Lao Tzu

Chapter Two: Where They Go

Three Theories

Knowing which winds blow the rainclouds can help you select your defenses. Bigger patterns of raincloud actions need more wind to keep the storm going. (If you can shut down the wind, the rainclouds lose power. Fewer winds mean fewer rainclouds.) There are shadings and layers to these winds, but I've found that there are three common forces that drive them. To keep things simple, I'll cheat and call them three theories.

Theory ONE: These are all a set of tricks to take over groups, and also to remove/cast out others, when someone feels there is competition for social "slots."

Theory TWO: Many of these tricks use fear to recruit others – to make others join their group, to avoid being attacked by that group. One of the reasons for grabbing slots and recruiting other people is the running decline rate of the raincloud groups. (Most people get tired of being nasty, fear based social pressure, or any mix thereof.)

Theory THREE: From time to time, the rainclouds feel a need to create publicity. In order to do this, they stir up trouble via blowing an event out of proportion. (Or even at times…*They make it up.*)

The Theory selects the Target

These three theories steer the rainclouds. The theories select the type of target, and the attack strategies they'll hit you with. The strategies are scripts: sets of words, actions and reactions that seem almost pre-recorded. If you listen carefully, you can spot the switch from how someone talks when they are just reacting, and the speech or phrases that they've learned and memorized. Some of the scripts the raincloud use include games of *incitement, whispering campaigns, shut down games, predators,* and *witch hunts.* To make it a little easier to see these game pieces, let's look at each for the following: targets, scripts, and actions. I've covered part of the idea of initial purposes under three theories.

Type ONE targets:

These tricks are used to take over groups. They are also used to remove/cast out others, when a faction feels there is competition for social 'slots.' Most type one arguments depend on slippery areas...type one attackers look for arguments where you can tone down critical skills, and play up social competition and identity. It's hard to take over technical based groups – technical skills are hard to argue with. Can you weld? Welding basics don't change about cultural perspective. The torch doesn't care if you are gay or straight. Can you fly a plane? Landing it safely proves your case. Radical groups like rainclouds don't have many applied technical skills, so they need to change the subject. They'll usually say that experience is a tool of oppression – maybe not directly, but you bet that they'll imply it.

Type TWO targets:

These tricks use fear to recruit others – coercing others into join their group, to avoid being attacked by that group. If you are in the public's eye, you may get lined up as the next type two target. Remember Matt Taylor, the Comet guy, back in 2014? He was the Project Scientist for the program that landed on a comet, and a bunch of whiners talked about his shirt "ruining" the landing for *them*. He gave a tearful TV apology. (The shirt was a gift from a graphic designer, and Comet guy was trying to help her via advertising.) That's a type two victory. One reason for grabbing slots and recruiting others is to slow down the steady loss of raincloud supporters. (Most people get tired of being nasty, dealing with fear based social pressure, tired of checking their friends' behavior for back sliding or back stabbing, or any mix of those three.) Either by fear, promising power, or even just a sense of nasty fun, these actions appeal by group status. If you join the group, the group (supposedly) won't attack you. The group offers you power, and members get to do things to other people. At least, that's the sales pitch.

Type THREE targets:

Movements need recurring publicity. It's their air supply. In order to get this, they stir up trouble by blowing an event out of proportion. Want to get thousands of people pissed off? Go to a university and spread rumors of hate symbols made from feces. The point is to get (and keep) people pissed off and acting before they think things through. You can spot how much a raincloud's been doing this, by how fast they start with the rhythmic chants and calls for fast group actions. Most of the time, you'll see a blend of these lens, snarled up to support each piece.

The choice of targets helps choose the script(s) used against that target. The choice of scripts chooses the order of those scripts. The goals of the attack and the type of targets all depend on ramping up emotional outbursts. These scripts share a set of roles, to play nasty games. The raincloud's noise level hides the roles they offer. Eric Dezenhall wrote *Nail 'Em!* to give a model that showed the roles. He described it as the "6V" model: Villain, Victim, Vindicator, Void, Value, and Vehicle. It's worth your time to read his book. The scripts need these V's covered. Missing any step means the raincloud can't get the attack rolling. As most of these depend on over the top drama, we can look tat hese steps like a cheesy movie. the basic raincloud game plan becomes: *The Oppressed, Villain, The Judge, Overcoming the Bad Thing in a Good Way*, and *The car that got us there.*

A valiant person who is OPPRESSED... all good raincloud scripts have an oppressed person. How can you have the oppressed rising up against injustice, without someone being Oppressed? (Later, the section on "Going Full Jesuit" shows a flaw in this idea...) If you can spot and avoid a person angling for that Oppressed victim role, you can save yourself a lot of pain. While your mileage may vary, and cultures tend to smear filters, here's **STABY** way to spot a predatory victim:

—Shock language (When you deal with the rainclouds, you will run into conversations that very quickly fall into the raincloud using obscenities to shock you.)

—Tries to piss you off (this is pretty much the whole point of being a raincloud – they aren't comfortable with logic and facts, so they try to keep you upset enough to have bad arguments. A great example is that slightly kinky/weird "I drink of your white tears" script.)

—Audience addiction (What would these rainclouds do without a web cam?) A lot of these games get played because the raincloud wants attention. When a raincloud can get any sort of reaction, they get to toddle off, skipping to the beat of:

Atten-tion!

Atten-tion!

I got

At-ten -tion!

—Brat, Yelling (is the person playing a game of "ain't it awful?" Are they carrying on like they are about to dissolve in a puddle of tears, or a pillar of fire? People over 18 are expected to act like an adult, and AVOID these kinds of behaviors.

A big reason for someone being in "victim mode" is to coerce others to change their behavior, or suffer social disapproval. Again, most actual victims of Trauma do not seek out public arenas to make a scene of their trauma. Most of actual survivors seek low attention, low stimulus areas – like quiet rooms with food. Rainclouds like the idea, but have to add drama. They need the attention that most survivors shun. Instead of seeing rainclouds as victims, picture them as foul mouthed clowns trying to drive a clown car. (Okay, maybe picture a cartoon raincloud with clown makeup. Whatever works for you...) The problem with Clown Cars is part of act is the car breaking down, or something getting run over. A close cousin to the *Victim* role is the 'defender' role – these turkeys try to 'speak for those without a voice' instead of just handing over the microphone/bullhorn to the supposed voiceless. Cry Bully: "You poor thing! You don't know that you have been brainwashed by the Oppressor!

Villain. We need our plucky victim/Hero to rise up against something, and fighting against a cheap caesar salad doesn't make a good script. We need a villain that can fire up the emotions. Also, the Villain should be explained with a scary few sound bites. When picking a Villain, we want to paint Villain as "strong," and "in power," but without too many social connections. The 'strength' of the Villain has to be beatable. (Ever notice how few times organized crime and gangs get targeted by the rainclouds? Picking a fight with a gang isn't healthy. Even rainclouds know that…) This is where things can go sideways. A group of rainclouds without a beatable villain gets cranky – but at each other. They need a string of wins to keep their own group momentum going – or they eat their own. There just aren't enough villains to go around. The Clowns have to hit something, or the clown car breaks down. This is why these social mugging games all **eventually** fail. (A bit later, I talk about how to build defenses.)

The Judge or *Validator* is the person stepping up to back the first lines in the plucky Victim's script. We need someone to confirm the *Victim* role. The more social clout the validator has, the more socially acceptable the hunting script becomes. "These studies by very important scholar in a different but related field say that I'm right!" The validators can cover up the big built in flaw in most raincloud arguments: *Privileges are the things that no one talks about.* Real privilege is the set of blind spots shared

30

by a culture. Someone that can gloss over this detail helps build/validate the rainclouds. Judges win by gaining some social authority. The judge/validator gains that social approval or authority from the rainclouds, by telling the rainclouds it's okay to use those scripts. This last piece can show the difference between Power and Force. The rainclouds are giving power for the judge. The judge then allows them to use force on others. If rainclouds need Judges to be "go time" cheerleaders, then short circuiting a Judge slows down the scripts – they have to find a new Judge. (I talk about defenses against the judges later.)

Cultures don't like to look at certain issues. If someone brings up one of those issues, people shift over to talking about something else. That's where *Overcoming a Bad Thing in a Good Way* come in. It gives people a way to deal with a thing they think is bad. All cultures create rules and habits to deal with things they find messy/bad, and those rules try to fix things early enough so that folks avoid seeing worse problems. This is one reason that rainclouds want to "start a conversation."

(SJW walks up to you in the bar): "We need to have a discussion about racism!"

You (confused): "I haven't said anything, my shirt has no saying on it…"

SJW: "It's an important issue that we need to talk about right now!"

31

They need the listener to hear about something that an ethical person would feel they have to fix. As of this writing, most of our culture (United States) regards Oppression as a bad thing. As long as the raincloud can link their rant to Oppression, they figure people will do what the raincloud asks, in order to stay away from that *Void*. *Value* is a quality that the Oppressed-Judge duet represent when they fight the *Villain*. The majority of cultures in the USA list bravery, justice, and competence as important *Values*. Getting into a punching match with somebody trying to bully you, showing non-violence at a peaceful protest, and getting into someone's face to declare when you feel some act or issue is wrong…Most people would say these actions are brave. Problems start showing up when the first style starts clashing with that third style. If someone uses negative stereotypes to attack you, you might be just a stand in character/punching bag for their cause - or neurosis. Rainclouds think their tantrums are brave. If you get targeted by rainclouds, it might be to show what badasses they are by silencing you.

The car that got us there is the raincloud's tool to move their arguments – the pieces of speech or concepts that show the victorious cry bullies heroically beating the bad things . This car needs three wheels to make it move: It's gotta be catchy, it's gotta have drama, and it's gotta show an act of *Value* beating down something bad.

Example: "When you talk about safety in cities, you aren't helping support the voiceless and struggling people in those cities."

This is the three wheeled car that the clowns drive. (Gotta have a car for the clowns to drive.) If you flatten one of its tires, then the car has trouble moving forward. (The counterattacks section goes into breaking the raincloud's car.)

"The pessimist complains about the wind; the optimist expects it to change; the realist adjusts the sails."
   William Arthur Ward, Writer

Chapter Three: What They Do...and How To Fight Back.

The best defenses revolve around *Security Culture.* That's when you get into the habit of listening to a group before you speak or act. While it sucks to turn down your own volume around a new crowd, it can be worth your while to step back and check how the winds blow. Check out the winds, before you sail into a group. If you can hear the Cry Bully talk for a while, they will point themselves out. Later on, when you've made friends and established your own group, the *Security Culture* mindset can help you avoid people that try to break up or take over your group.

If you missed seeing the storm clouds, or decided to walk in anyway, more active measures will need to happen. The raincloud is pissing you off and the storm is brewing.

Back in the mid 1930's, there was a guy named Alan Monroe, who sat down and outlined how to persuade people into a five step process: *Get* Their Attention, *Show* there's a problem, *Give* your solution, *Tell* them the other solutions are wrong, and then *Call* them to action. (I'm bastardizing a lot, but I'm crunching it down to save space.)

The first step is to *Get their Attention*. They need to say something to quickly hook their target. This is when you check if you are THE target, or A target. If the language goes south fast, they aren't trying to win you over. They want to shut you up or they are trying to scare the crowd (there's almost always a crowd – that's a sign.)

Show there's a problem. This step is when they ramp up emotions. To get this going, they'll keep angling to get everybody else pissed off – logic be damned. Rainclouds want to link their problem to your hot buttons as quick as they can. (You aren't straight, you're cis-het, and probably scum. If you disagree, you are using your privilege to oppress them, or that if you disagree you are showing you are the problem etc, etc, ad fucking nauseam.) Rainclouds will edit and manufacture the truth when they feel pushed. They will build up the problem with phrases like "their lived experiences can't be ignored." Interestingly enough, their lived experiences override other people's lived experiences. The rainclouds have damn near made an industry of creating their own expert(s) and group(s) to validate their experiences and narratives. This gets them a running stream of new Judges to validate the raincloud's Hunting. The rainclouds act/sound authoritative about some deep need/void with this stream. If you can short-circuit the "authorities," you can pull the wind from

35

their sails. ("You're gonna quote Luce Irigaray? Isn't she the nutbar that thought E=MC^2 was sexist? I don't see any reason to bring her mental illness into your conversation…") It means you have to know something about their "authorities" but it's easy enough to ask: w"hat does (semi-famous 'authority') have to do with my actions?" "Why should I care?" Do yourself a favor and look through "the 69 non material needs" from *The Book of Visions*, and figure out which speak to you. Then build a set of guard covers over each of those. If you feel yourself getting heated at the raincloud really fast, that's the first roll of thunder – if you hear it for what it is, you can just close things up, walk away, and stay dry. An important step on the raincloud's list is linking up their "piss-you-off" statements to each of the steps. That's the start of the wind. Usually, these characters will use logical fallacies to keep the emotional charge going – and that's the rain. (A little further along, I cover the most common logical fallacies.)

Give their solution. This is where the raincloud gives you the chance to be a Good Person. You want to be a Good Person, don't you? All you have to do is follow their guidance. Is that so much to ask? If they aren't handing out a solution that you can pull off, they're playing for the crowd. Wanna really mess with them? Right after their solution step, say "that's fine, but I don't care, and you no longer get to speak to me in any form." (I cover a little more of this under the No-Stop-Go Away section). A few less final methods can include phrases like "I certainly understand that you could feel that way," "I understand, but don't agree," and just looking at them a for a few moments, muttering "hmmm," and then go back to what you were doing.

Tell them the other solutions are wrong, and the raincloud's solution is right. Just think of it! As soon as you realize how wrong you are – and start making those changes - the sooner you can be a Good Person. Just think of the better world we will all have, as soon as you stop being so stubborn! (That was hard to say with a straight face…) This is a great combat zone, if you want to fight for the middle ground. Many rainclouds running Monroe's five steps will feel a need to silence any critics at this point. They use the term "derail" for a reason. If you keep pointing out the raincloud's solution is bad, or that we've already got a solution for the problem they've been going on about…their little rage choo-choo jumps off the tracks.

Call them to action. Gee, you're not up and enthusiastic about the raincloud's new plan. Obviously, the raincloud needs to stoke the emotions again. They need to call you out some more, so that your better self will join their noble quest! The simple and more obvious versions for the call to action step use lots of action verbs (Join, Tell, Fight, Stand Up, etc). Less obvious versions use a variation on the "yes set" - an argument built on the idea that people are creatures of habit, and will agree to things if they've said yes to a string of previous statements that they can agree with. More complex versions attempt to build implied agreements into a target's definite acceptance.

We've looked at the Ideologies that provide target selection and which script the attackers might best use. Many of these scripts need "triggers" to signal the start of the script. Some of these 'green lights' are reactive (Dog whistle words), some are proactive (Virtue Signaling), and some are used to link up to and hijack an existing conversation (Word Fogging). These triggers start *games*. Look, there are many possible counters to these behaviors, but for expediency's sake, I'll just give you a single example. But you aren't limited to the examples.

Simple Games

Dog Whistle Words are the script and reactions when the raincloud gets hurt over your words.

In society, there are terms that are generally accepted as offensive. You don't normally use them unless you intend to give offense. Also, if you accidently give offense, you apologize.

Having said that, also know: Every group has a list of icons and concepts that they find uncomfortable it ties in with #4 *Void*. That's one of the things that helps define said group. If the group is big enough, not using certain terms in mixed company is an accepted social 'rule.'

Dog Whistle words interrupt these normal patterns

When someone is complaining about a common word, they mare playing with Dog Whistles – the complainer hears something that other people can't hear.

Example:"People using the term 'Thug' as a negative word…that sounds racist to me…"

Someone complaining about something doesn't actually mean there is something to be heard. It could mean the complainer has issues "normal" people don't relate to This is not uncommon. The question is how much do you want do deal with that? Is it worth your time and effort to work things out with this person? You have every right to ask these questions and decide.

Raincloud like to force changes on others.

They're not just looking for an excuse to get offended, they go out of their way to hear insults and wrongs in normal words. This gives them the excuse to bully others into changing. Again, they'll come at you through your desire not to be rude, but especially your not wanting to hurt people. Your cruel and cutting words hurt their sensitive little doggie ears. In any case, this script can be a great starter piece to "engage in conversations" about the raincloud's favorite "cry of the heart" topic (cis-normality, privilege, 'safety' overriding rights, etc.)

There's always going to be a sliding scale for this sort of thing. You can gauge this script by asking: Do I get the feeling that the person in question is trying to change of my words, or does it feel like they are trying to change ME?

A person tinsisting your use of ordinary words is hurting them...is a person trying to change a lot more than your words.

The best way to deal with this tactic is to…

KEEP NAILING YOUR POINTS DOWN

Use solid dictionary definitions. Don't accept non-standard definitions, unless you've really looked into the subject. Don't follow the raincloud's attempts to redefine your words. When they try to claim that a conservative comment is like a reactionary comment, which is like a racist comment, nail your points down. Point out that what they did is a logical fallacy known as a "slippery slope" argument. Point out they are engaging in rhetoric, not logic, when they use these tactics (Rhetoric is a collection of tricks of speech. Logic is founded on rational arguments, built on facts). If they start in with "the so called 'standard definition' is a tool of the Oppressor," you're within your rights to wish them a festive May Day and a triumphant October. (That's being snarky, and the rainclouds might miss a bit of the snark...but either way, have some fun with it.)

Virtue Signaling shows the things a culture thinks are important.

To keep it really quick: *Virtue Signaling* is when somebody makes a statement promoting an active social cause (Gay Marriage, Veganism, Gun Control/Rights, Save the Whatevers, etc). The statement question has to show a "call to action" flavor. A sticker that states "I like Fettecini Alfredo" isn't much of a Virtue Signal. A sticker that says "I'm eating Fettecini Alfredo for Social Justice!" IS a Virtue Signal

Virtue Signaling serves many purposes. First, it's to show loyalty to a cause or group with those words ("I like Fettecini Alfredo.") Second, Virtue Signals act like a beacon to find other people that feel the same way ("Hey…You like Fettecini Alfredo? So do I!") Third, it's to take over a conversation. If no one is talking about something, and you keep bringing it up in casual conversation, you can slowly make that the topic of conversation – and maybe change the actions of the speakers ("I remember that we talked about Fettecini Alfredo last week, so I made us a pot full…") Fourth, Virtue Signals can act like a conversational trip wire. When you disagree with the speaker, you placed yourself in the *Villain* role. Virtue signaling scripts linked up with the *word fogging* script can quickly go off the deep end. ("How dare you say you don't like Fettecini! Why are you trying to erase an entire culture? Have you no feelings about others at all?")

The rainclouds usually will keep amping up their signals until you respond. A great trick to deal with this is to respond, but show that you won't be side tracked itno their script. Act like a *Broken Record* and get back to your own activities: Say something like "...Sorry to hear that…" (in the same tone of voice you'd use to give a kiss off line to a crackhead,) and go back to your conversation. Repeat as needed. If you don't engage with them, they can't get their points. A pricklier version is the cold shoulder: When they say something to you, calmly inform them you just don't care. When they call you heartless, again turn and inform that you just don't care - and go back to your earlier pursuits. When they put out a trap, look at them and tell them that you just don't care. (There are legions of memes playing on "I do not give a fuck what you say." Find one, work with it, and use it with style and grace.)

Word Fogging is when a person builds up an argument, or a piece of an argument, from easily misunderstood terms.

The goal of *Word Fogging* is to slide into the previous point: flexible definitions help slide a normal conversation into tripwires and virtue signals. A great example of *Word Fog* is the term "Gender identity." Does the term "gender" mean the plumbing one was born with? Does it mean "looking like the agreed upon appearance that matches a person with said plumbing?" Who gets to define "identity?" The phrase gets murky very quickly. Consider another example: "Family Values." Whose family, and whose values?

"It means what I say it means" is a remix of that Word Fogging. It starts with the standard definition of a word, and then slowly blurs that term into a new meaning that meets the needs of the Raincloud. Most of the games from the raincloud's playbook are built on the idea of getting you to buy into their worldview. They can't make people do anything, unless other people believe that the raincloud is "right." One of the ways rainclouds try to do this is by changing those definitions.

You would think if you don't buy into the raincloud's worldview, then all they are doing is whining and complaining that people should listen to them – in other words, they sound like a spoiled child, except these spoiled children often throw temper tantrums when you don't buy in.

Instead of buying into the "bad guy" role of automatically disagreeing with them, try *confusing* them at first. Don't give the raincloud an opening for a response line. Instead, respond by first saying things unconnected to what the raincloud says. As an example, think of the following exchange:

Raincloud: I feel offended by your comment!

YOU: I'm sorry, but I've already paved my local street with shaved chocolate…

Raincloud: You need to stop oppressing me!

YOU: correct me if I'm wrong, but the panel on the fish slapping dance doesn't start until later tonight…

Raincloud: You are disrespecting and offending me!

YOU: Why yes, my telephone IS bright yellow!

This kind of thing takes a lot of "on your toes thinking" so a quick shortcut to make this work is to make unusual observations: "nope…there's still a lot of shoes…" and go back to your original conversation, minus the raincloud. If they persist, use this trick again, and immediately follow it up with nailing your points down, and then get right back to your conversation. (This tells the raincloud that they are wrong, that you don't care about their opinion, and you aren't going to get hooked into the roles they try to lay out.)

Complex Games

    Complex games require more effort, and usually need more rainclouds for the team. These more complex scripts help call/create swarms of rainclouds. As rainclouds tend to be personal cowards but brave members of a group. Therefore, rainclouds try to scale up to these as quick as they can. These games include *Incitement games, Whisper campaigns, Shut down games, Predators, Swarms,* and the often mentioned *Witch Hunts.*

People use *Incitement Games* to piss someone off enough to get ousted "for rash behavior."

The raincloud quietly says things to "push people's buttons" until the person react in a way that the group won't like. Then the raincloud starts making louder comments comments that show why the target is obviously the bad guy. Flustered, the target often makes the mistake of getting madder and louder - which plays into the incitement trap.

Examples include:

"You can't speak here!"

"I think you are a FASCIST for promoting police procedures!"

It might be considered a form of entrapment – the raincloud is going out of their way to piss a target off, and then get their target kicked out. That's using a group to eject someone that they don't like, without being upfront about it. This also happens pretty often. People learn this one in grade school. It usually isn't much of a gamble – most times – for the raincloud. The rainclouds only do this when they feel it won't snap back on them.

Rage Monkey is a great way to counter this. It shows the raincloud that their game is going to snap back on them. You aren't getting angry, and you aren't just letting them push you around. Use phrases like "You seem upset…" "Why are you so upset…" "You really seem upset…" (repeat as needed). No matter what they say, ask if they are upset. It will take a while to get them hooked in, but you can have them screaming that they are most emphatically not upset. This loses their social support. Another way to push the Rage Monkey is calling out the shut down artist, and then calmly breaking down their other argument points. ("Hey! Raincloud! Did you just try a shut down game? That's kind of a dick move! It sounds like you're trying to cover up your mistakes.")

Whisper campaigns are character assassination, and little else. They spread false evidence by quietly speaking to new people. The hope is to gain a convert, get the message spread, or to at least shut up other people. It's rarely presented as a direct statement that points from the attacking raincloud to the target - "John said that Mary stole his car." Instead, this one shows up as "I heard that Tommy said that they'd heard Mary had stolen John's car, and I see no reason to believe that they'd lie…" This one can destroy careers and remove social access. (Look up

"SJW" and "fired." Look up "The Honey Badger Brigade.") The raincloud can also attempt to avoid discussing some issues by creating rumors and spreading that fact that there are rumors about the topic. This is used as a threat campaign: the rainclouds will use this, if you speak against them.

There's a flip side to this one: by describing all of the accusations pointed against the raincloud-favored groups as rumors, the rainclouds can side track some people from looking too closely at those groups – forget about the sources or the evidence. This method works really well with a bought/rigged media system, because the only way the public can learn about the actual facts is by looking into those "wild rumors" via the sources that naming those events as "rumors." Whenever a raincloud has an opening, they introduce new scripted "facts" or clues to mess up an opponent's presentations. This can short circuit conversations (or resolutions) about sensitive issues. This works best when the "crime" being talked about deals with "facts" that aren't be easily separated from opinions and fabrications. Any case built on two sets of opposing statements ("he/she said"), is ripe for a whisper campaign.

Whisper campaigns need that easy or tired target for their fuel. Rainclouds use these campaigns to grab and build power networks by showing strength – a la the "do what I say, or you get it like Johnny did" - or even a more subtle "I'm the only one you can trust who will tell you just how bad Johnny is" *Lord of The Rings* Grima Wormtoungue style. Combine these two, and it can get ugly.

The most direct way to short circuit a whispering campaign is to publicly confront the whisperer, loudly. Point out the facts of the matter. Deny their "logical" links that try to connect actual facts to the whisperer's narrative. Shame the foulness of their rumors. Use low key or high drama, but make sure other people see you winning (or at least not losing) the confrontation. Put out the calmest vibe you can, but make sure that others publicly hear and see you doing the confrontation. But know, if you do this, the rumor monger may then move on to a *Shutdown game.*

Shutdown games are some of the easiest to see, and to deal with, but they are often used as a Hail Mary pass. The raincloud will say something meant to shame the other party into silence. Most shut down games are built on making someone feel bad or stupid. This can range from simple ones like "Only an idiot or a junkie would believe that. Which are you?" to the more fake but smart sounding "Your actions are built on your flawed analysis of my deep and profound writings that regard post/meta modernism in the field of the eternal subjunctive, as seen in the inherent power inequalities of Little Bo Peep…" This approach just oozes condescension and superiority. That, more than the exact words is what emotionally triggers people and makes them fall for this tactic. If you weren't so upset you'd realize what the person is saying makes no sense (word fogging.)

All shutdown games are an attempt to force the target into a lower or submissive role. If you don't roll with the masters and servants crowd, don't buy into the role. First, verbally point out what they are doing. ("Hey Raincloud! Was that a Shutdown game? Why are you trying to shut down the conversation I was having?") Then exclude them from conversation. If the raincloud persists, use *No-stop-go away-tell* – Most groups/institutions have a rule that says that if someone says a version of those words, your interactions with them are done. Learn that rule and use it. If your conversation is interrupted/disrupted by one of these folk, turn and say – especially publicly – to them "No, I do not want to talk with you. Stop talking to me. Go away from me." Then move 20 feet (seven or so long paces) away from them. If they walk over to you, tell the local authority that said raincloud is harassing you, and you wish to file a complaint/charges. (Understand something: rainclouds will always lie to serve their cause. Make sure that you've either recorded the conversation, or get to the security guys before the raincloud.) By the group's rules, the other person is a harasser, and said person now faces whatever penalties the group dishes out. Taking this action is going hardcore, and one of you is probably leaving. If the group decides to support the raincloud, it's better that you leave anyway.

Predators

As in nature, there are different forms of predators/social muggers. There are aggressive ones that chase their targets (Wolves), quieter ones that slowly whittle away your objections and poison your personal drive (Snakes), and the social web builders that try and bind you into not saying no (Spiders).

Wolves are the best known predators in our culture. TV, movies, far too many Internet groups…All of our shared scripts and media tropes help demonstrate this predator. This is the classic "Won't take no for an answer" type. In an earlier dating and courtship culture, they were called mashers. In the dating world, politics, or business, the Wolves pick someone and chase that target down. Wolves are the ones in the protest world screaming in people's faces. They are the ones willing to get recorded calling for mob violence against certain "privileged" people, due to the taken-as-faith sin of "privilege." They are also the ones likely to *act* on mob violence. (Google "AntiFa," "Yvette Felarca," and "Black Bloc." For Right Wing groups, there's always looking at Southern Poverty Law Center for hate crimes.) Compared to the other types of predators, they are strangely refreshing. Wolves usually stick with Shutdowns and Incitement games. A great way to deal with wolves is to practice *Attention overload.* Give the raincloud the attention that they raincloud want. Welcome back to class! The Raincloud is now your favorite professor on your favorite topic, and you feel you must learn everything about the topic! Everything!

E V E R Y T H I N G!

Think about how un-nerving having one person – in close quarters – pay ALL of their attention to you. Try to think of the raincloud as the perfect guru...and first new meal for the starving man...and the sexiest thing you can picture. Roll that all up into one emotion. Now try to look at the raincloud with that in mind. Now get all your friends to do the same thing. "What do you mean you're leaving? Come back!" Pay attention: do NOT follow the person, as that could be considered stalking.) At the very worst, you can learn a lot more of their thinking style, and therefore learn their weaknesses. (A wise sailor adjusts his sails...) Warning: many rainclouds have long term abuse and/or neglect issues. A number of them have personality disorders and/or substance abuse issues as well. Actually and dramatically paying attention to them might either cause them to increase the level of attack (up to physical), or just the opposite. They may decide that you are "the only person who understands them."

Snakes work on their prey's emotions and self-esteem. The snake is quiet and methodical, and most charm their way out

51

of almost anything. (This one has some limits, however... As they say "it works great, until it crashes and burns.") Snakes put their target on an emotional roller coaster to keep the target from having enough time or mental/emotional space to cool down and think things through. (Unfortunately, this type of "social guidance" also rolls down a dark trail to abusive situations faster than you can shake a stick.) If you are starting to feel guilty or bad about yourself for saying no, you might be dealing with a Snake. The Wolf wants you feel to defensive/threatened, the Snake wants you to feel guilty. They'll use the same tricks as the Wolf, but prefer to soften it with either loaded questions or whisper campaigns.

Example:"How does it feel to know that people supporting you are alt-right fascists?"

Sometimes, the best thing to do is just *Laugh* at the CHORFs (Cliquish Holier-than-Thou Obnoxious Reactionary Fanatic). It will probably piss them off, but it can build an emotional barrier. The ranter is going to rant louder. Great. Embrace the suck. If you can keep laughing while they rant, you win – laughing at them switches the tone. It makes it that much harder for the raincloud to show you are shamed. When you are done with laughing, either leave, or get ready to keep engaging your opponent. As a side note, you might want to weigh the benefits and the cost of engaging in any way with these turkeys. If you have the opportunity to walk away, that may be the best choice. Walking away, avoiding, or ignoring the rainclouds can bypass most problems. These versions of all follow the "Don't start none, won't be none" ethos. Laughing at a CHORF may get them to press their attack, but "calling out" each logical fallacy or trick used by the ranting CHORF will piss them off. A fun game for laughing at SJWs is a game sometimes called SJW BINGO. There are truck loads of internet pictures floating around that show a variation of a Bingo card with very smart sounding academic and/or CHORFy type sayings/terms. Either grab up some from the net, or make your own. Hand them out to friends (but perhaps only those friends you trust. Some rainclouds will try to use this kind of thing against you via a Kafka-trap or some sort of DARVO – Deny Assault Reverse Victim Offender. A Kafka-trap is when an accuser uses denial of guilt as proof of guilt. When you hear the terms used, you then have a choice: You can walk away (Evasion), *Laugh* at them, or counter attack (maybe by yelling "Bingo!"), which can disrupt the other person's rant. The point of keeping it in a game form is to provide a mental pause, a step back, from the emotional tantrums of the raincloud. Another point for keeping it game like is also to provide a running "score." More points would suggest a greater and greater reason to evade the possible raincloud.

Spiders (and their webs) are a real bastard to deal with. Spiders prefer to create situations to entrap their prey. Spiders build webs of social contacts, and then let other people run through social approval games to bring the Spider a crop of new victims. Spiders keep appealing to group feelings/ethics to steer the behavior of everyone. "If we believe in this, then we have to go and do..." is the working "logic" here. If you want to get fancy/erudite, you could say that the Spiders are attempting to rewrite the local active narrative. If you aren't that highbrow, they subtly twist the mission of the group and rely on fear of being called a hypocrite to keep people from calling them out on what they're doing.

A few scripts that the spiders might use include:

->"I'm sure you didn't mean to disagree with so-and-so, as he is just fighting for <insert the most favored cause here> and I'm SURE you aren't against <cause>. Why don't you just apologize to so-and-so, and we can all get back to business."

->"But you simply CAN'T say no to helping Henrietta. If you do, you'll just be making her feel bad, like all the others..."

->But you've already agreed to my first three points, so you MUST agree with my fourth and fifth points. How can you say no to joining our group, and still be a good person?

Get yourself untangled from these webs of "logic" and run the hell away. However, if you are trying to protect your community, job, etc, you might need to respond. As Spiders work by trying to sound so very reasonable in their attacks, a great response is to use "reason" against them. Coolly debate them point by point. I call this one *Going Jesuit*. One stereotype of a Jesuit is the dude who calmly sets fire to stupid arguments. Use your favorite search engine and look up Louis Reykhauser. Then look up Star Trek original series. Concentrate on Mr. Spock That's the vibe you want. Sort of a "Mr. Spock is oh so very tired of your shit." Try to follow that script when you calmly and coolly debate that Spider – going after their argument line by line. Actively look for, and take apart, the errors in their speech. That's debating. When you look at a debate – a real one, not the kind where people throw chairs – there are 4 basic rules:

> Rule Zero: Don't Lose your cool – try to get them to lose theirs.
> Rule One: Don't buy into their frames – poke holes in that frame.
> Rule Two: Don't buy into unsupported "definitions" or "facts" as independent points.
> Rule Three: Don't buy into faulty "logic."

Don't lose your cool. The whole point for the social muggers, is for you to lose your cool – they want you scared, pissed off, or ashamed. (Hmmm…again, what kind of person does that sound like…) When they talk, breathe in like a reverse yawn. This blocks out a lot of their tone, and it makes them look silly – some of the rainclouds can lose it, if you do this one. Remember that most rainclouds are counting on you getting and staying angry. If you can keep calmly debating them, they get bored, mad, or threatened. They may try to build a hunt against you, but losing their momentum makes it harder for them to "win." As mentioned earlier, people only have a certain amount of grit when keeping up a fight they feel they can't win – or don't care about the prizes.

Don't buy into their frame – If you haven't committed a crime, YOU are not the problem. Crybullies (from basic garden variety rainclouds to full on witch hunting mobs) want you to guilt/fear trip yourself into to doing something for that raincloud - and that guilt truip they want you to buy into has no reward of "thank you" for you. Dig it: The rainclouds have no automatic "right" to guilt trip you. Is the raincloud a cop or government official, making a lawful request? Do they employ you? Do you have a relationship with them? Do you owe them money? Have you already agreed to do something for them or your community (including background social rules of the group that you are a part of)? Do you want to be friends with this person? If the answers are no, then you are being patient in talking with the raincloud. You don't have to be endlessly patient. Yelling at them is a short lived pleasure. Politely telling them to hop into the piranha tank can be a lot more fun. The same idea happens to be true, when looking at how the rainclouds try to frame other arguments. If they claim that skills don't matter, call them on that. They want to accuse someone? The burden of proof is on the accuser. Ask yourself why you aren't allowed to question the "proof" that you oppress others... Then ask the raincloud why you can't question their "proof." One definition of privilege is being in a position where others aren't allowed to question your role. If someone else can question your role, it isn't a privileged role. If someone attacks you for having privilege, but will not let you question the evidence, that person is showing privilege. If they are supposedly fighting those with privilege, why are they showing that same flavor of power/privilege? That' sounds like hypocrisy.

Don't buy into unsupported "facts." A bunch of the more >ahem< "logic" based arguments that the rainclouds will trot out start with a quote or a number they propose as an accepted fact (and usually a very scary number...), or they haul out their pie charts blaring some emotional horror show that absolutely needs fixing right now. What's their source? Is it valid? Is it related? Do you care? Does the "fact" have any relevance to their argument or your goals? If the "facts" they are trying to sell use a lot of loaded language, then there's probably some "reinterpretation of facts." As an example: consider articles involving police involved shootings. Does a source describe all police related shootings as "shootings" or "murder?" Do "studies" listed by this source describe "mob violence" or "militant activity?" Are actual definitions ever mentioned?

Don't buy into faulty "logic." Hear logical fallacies from the REASONS list? Point them out, and them calmly go back to your own conversation. They brought up another logical fallacy? Point out that one as well. (Fun fact: Rainclouds *hate* when you call them on their fallacies.) A real logical argument starts with facts, shows their truth, connects up other facts, and then tests the whole thing to find out what happens next. Rainclouds need to get people to agree to their braand of insanity. That means they need to shut down logical error correction. They need to use logical fallacies (another name for errors in logic) to make this happen. When I used to teach, I created an acronym I called **REASONS** to help students remember the most common logical fallacies: **R**ed Herring, **E**motional Appeal, **A**ppeal to Authority, **S**trawman, **O**nly two, **N**o one knows, and **S**lippery slope. While describing each, I'll add a few counters and how to user them. (Yes, I know I'm not using the right names for the fallacies, this is a memory-tool. Deal.)

Red Herring – One of the biggest versions of this is a game called "distract by different argument" If you go for this, it's off to the races with moving goal-posts. This is a "win" for them. Instead, ask "what does your new point have to do with the earlier conversation?" Or give them a cheery "whatever" and go back to whatever you were doing.

Emotional Appeal has four main flavors: the *Appeal to Force*, *Appeal to Fear*, *Appeal to Pity*, and *Appeal to Gallery*. Appeal to Force – this one is in the background a lot. The raincloud will rarely directly threaten you (for a whole bunch of reasons), but the threat is always in the background. Mind you, they will try and flip it so that YOU are the bad guy who threatens THEM (and then they will start making an *Appeal to Gallery*). *Appeal to Fear* – if you don't agree/go along with, the bad guys win – or something bad happens to you. In the case of the raincloud using you as a target, there's always the chance it's not personal, and that said raincloud is trying to put a scare into other people. Think about that, if you roll with the Sheepdog code. (If they attack the sheepdog, how much worse will it be for the sheep? Defend yourself…defend the flock.) *Appeal to Pity* – please, think of the children! (Or the puppies! Or the green things..). If you don't agree with the attacker, you are a Bad Person. *Appeal to Gallery* is where they talk/speak to "win the room." The whole point of the rainclouds is to shame others, frighten people into joining their cult, and take over groups. When you short-circuit an appeal to gallery, their attack fails quickly. If you are willing to deal with the waves, you can use this against them quite nicely – but beware the pushback (no ham actor likes losing the spotlight). Adding the pieces together make a great tool to provoke a response (take an appeal to force with a hook for an appeal to gallery, staple that to a negative stereotype, and then add a trap if you disagree). Ask yourself, what are you going to gain from talking to the raincloud? What's the cost? Do you want this trade? This one can act like a social thermometer. Check out how much the rest of your community agrees.

Appeal to Authority includes two flavors, the Appeal to Invisible Authority - "they" won't let you – and the Appeal to Mis-placed Authority – where the attacker uses one higher profile figure to fill in for another. A great example of mis-placed authority was an old commercial from the late 70's with the winning quote of "I'm not a doctor, but I play one on TV, and..."

The *Straw Man* fallacy is simple: Make the other guy look like an idiot for suggesting something – the raincloud will take your position off to the deep end. As an example: "Sunny days are good." "If all days were sunny, we'd never have rain, and without rain, we'd have famine and death." Your response can have blowback. A low stress response would be say something like "no, that's not what I said…" restate your original position, and then continue whatever you were doing before the raincloud blew into your life. Understand that going nuclear may offer satisfaction, but you're still standing in the rain. ("Hey Raincloud! Why you so insecure that the only way you feel you can push your point is by making cheap shot attacks on dumbed down versions of what I said? Can you at least address the points I actually made?") Ask yourself if you *must* stand in that rain. The raincloud will keep pushing to get you emotional. The smarter ones will try to tease you into defending a straw man they put out. If the raincloud can keep you pissed off, they are likely to start turning the conversation over to talking about how overly sensitive you are. (They aren't being abusive…oh no…it's you showing "fragility" or "privilege." The Kafka traps can abound with this one…)

The *Only Two* fallacy tries to focus the target's choice to only two choices. If you go to an ice cream parlor, and you see more than two choices, but the server only wants to serve two flavors…you're dealing with an *Only Two* situation. Some *Only Two* fallacies are pressure fronts the rain clouds slide around on: Gun Control, Abortion, Immigration, Capitalism, Free speech/Speech codes, etc. By pointing out alternatives, you weaken their argument. In an ice cream store, there are usually more flavors than just chocolate or vanilla. How about a scoop of pistachio or mint?

No One Knows…If you don't have contrary evidence, right now, the rain cloud must be right. (They will probably demand that you apologize for your error – don't.) Look, you haven't SEEN any evidence proving UFOs don't exist, right? That must mean there is no evidence that they don't exist, right? That means we just haven't found the evidence that they exist, right? That's how this fallacy works. (…and Nessie, Elvis, and I will be over there, having pistachio ice cream).

Slippery Slope arguments state that actions cause other actions, which slide down into some horrible doom. This one links up with Straw man fallacies. The euthanasia arguments show these Slippery Slopes. If you allow assisted suicide, then it's only a matter of time until the government runs death camps.

There are another 36 basic fallacies out there, but these seven are the most used – hell, they're overused past the point of satire. After a while, when hearing these muggers talk/scream the same scripts, it's almost pleasant to hear someone use one of the others like No True Scotsman, or Alternative Advance, or a good rousing chain of Argument from Hearsay.

By using these "Jesuit" rules, you can take a mental step back from the verbal spittle/rain that the rainclouds pour forth. Instead, you can take each word the raincloud gives you as an opportunity to fight for the middle ground.

For a real rat bastard of a day, think about those new social campaigns created to help stop assaults (a noble goal). These groups are targeting what they consider Wolves, but they are ignoring the Snakes and Spiders.

Another side note: when you look at groups, you are going to find people trying to buy into relationship with that group. Some people try to buy into a group by 'dating' the Spider. Spiders are good at networking (hence the nickname). When Spiders attack (excuse me, "when spiders defend themselves from Oppression") they gather their contacts to make a group oriented strike (please pardon that misspelling – I meant "militant defense.") Like stinging insects, these characters move in a Swarm.

Swarms

If a social situation is starting to see Swarms, then it's a pretty good guess that a group of Cry bullies has decided that they've got a good chance of throwing their weight around and grabbing big chunks of power from a group. like rainclouds in real life can gather together and become bigger storms, Cry Bullies can gather together to try and cause trouble. The whole point of a swarm is to make the rainclouds look scary. They are either trying to use the threat of violence, or are trying use bandwagon style arguments – the more the speakers, and the louder they are, the more the rainclouds must be right…Right? (By the way the rainclouds rarely get actually physically violent. If a group of rainclouds is moved from yelling nd threatening to actually assaulting people, that swarm has turned into a Witch Hunt. More on that in just a bit.) Swarms think this actually works. A dangerous thing about swarms is that the members start to lose their own perspective. They don't "see" other people as individuals – they "see" people as stand-in members of another group. One member of the hated group can quickly replace another. This kind of thing has gang warfare and racist hate crimes written all over it. It just depends on who is in the mob, and who survives to complain. Usually, swarms gather together, yell a hell of a lot to blow off steam, and then leak away in dribs and drabs. The problem is that they can clump together even more than just a swarm. The Swarms can jumble together and build themselves up into a rolling hate engine – in other words, they rile themselves themselves up to go witch hunting.

Evasion is the art of winning the fight by not being in one. The best way to avoid getting rained on is avoiding being under any clouds. Hearing certain words in a group's conversation is like watching a cloud form. If you notice those words thrown around, you can walk away and avoid the fight. At the time of this writing, these are a few of the words to watch out for: *Advocate, Agent, Agency, Ally, Dialogue, Dominant Culture, Fragility,*

Intersectionality, Internalized-, Marginalized, Naming,
Oppression, People Of Color, Privilege, Problematic, Safe Space,
Social Justice, Silencing, Spotlighting, and *Triggering.* Keeping a
mental list provides better security, but perhaps not as much fun -
instead, make a physical checklist and compare the background
speeches with that list. Like a being in real boat, spotting
rainclouds on the horizon and steering clear means you avoid
getting rained on. I believe people should warn others about
storms/muggers. If the group supports the rainclouds, then there's
a chance that you're looking at a thunderhead or worse, and a
wise sailor avoids choppy weather. Steer clear and warn the
others. (Stick to facts only, as some folks get sue-happy).

Witch Hunts

Witch Hunts are simple and easy to explain: they blow off
social steam by going after a scapegoat (or a set of folks forced
into the class role of scapegoats), sliding down from a socially
prominent target to an easy one. It's built up as a weapon, and it
can occur "naturally" in stressed out social groups.

The difference between a Witch Hunt, and a bunch of
uptight weirdos screaming "kill the pig!" is pretty simple: Witch
Hunts try to stay in the form of "Avenging a Wrong/killing evil."
They act a lot like storms, and can sometimes be avoided as such.

Witch Hunts have a pre-set of list of roles – it's like an

evil fast food place with greasy picture push button menus. There are opportunities for multiple Witch Hunters (you can sometimes have status fights for who gets to be the head of the Witch Hunters). There has to be a witch – at least one. (A large and shadowy force of evil, revealing itself one or two at a time is much better. Even better is to have the witches be not socially prominent or loners.) Sometimes, if the group needs the skills of one Witch, they may offer a chance to recant. (You say that you're wrong, offer to do some sort of penance, and then you can rejoin the group.) In longer running games, you can sometimes see onetime Witches as Witch Hunters. There has to be someone willing to agree with/validate the witch hunters that they too think that there is a witch. The person validating the witch hunt may be trying to "switch the witch," may be caught up in the emotional furor, or might even be seeing a chance to gain some power. (Switch the witch is the attempt to point the mob at another target.)

Fighting back against Witch Hunts takes a lot of time and energy - and sometimes even takes a lot of money. Take a good look at the group that has a Witch Hunt rampaging around. Is the group "worth it" to you? Why? Remember that here are differences between the non regulated "social world" and business/law/politics. If you feel that you need to stay and deal with a Witch Hunt, here's a few guidelines to help you defend yourself, and fight the hunters.

Keep costing them victories

Short circuit the narrative

Short-circuit the drama

Undermine the judge

Dropping the hammer

Keep costing them victories

Groups playing games need to feel like they have a chance to win - why play the game, if it's rigged against you? Every game has to have a payoff. The more you can shake up that "we can win" feeling, the more members will leave the Witch Hunt . When they lose "enough" members, the Witch Hunt slides back down the outrage slope to being smaller swarms, then a huffy little group, and finally some lone spoiled brat whining on about how they didn't get their way. Witch Hunts need that constant stream of "victories" to build their momentuum, and to build and maintain their group. Each time they lose at something, they lose the horsepower to push their story. Each time they lose a member, they have fewer voices to push that story. When a Witch Hunt attacks, look for the heaviest weight attacker. When they speak, directly point out where their accusations are wrong. When the next person chimes in, ask who gets paid for them pushing this Witch Hunt? That likely will cause howls of denial. When they then try to redirect their attacks, again point where they are wrong, and then ask what purpose does it serve for them to keep pushing lies? Witch Hunts need to feel that their attacks are moral victories. Their narratives can't live without believing that they can win, that their victories are "moral," and that other people will think of the Hunters as virtuuous..

.

Short circuit the narrative

All Witch Hunts are based on a dramatic story. The more the members of the Hunt get to yell and bay at the moon, the better. Narratives need a storyline (one that and momentum - they need time to pick up speed. If you can keep pointing out where the narrative is wrong, the Hunters need to find a way to patch up their story. Most narratives are not about reality. Instead, most narratives are a reflection of someone's interpretation of reality The fact that New York City had filed for bankruptcy in 1975 is a fact grounded in reality. Saying that political and finanical leaders in New York City were foolish in their spending habits is an interpretation of reality. Stating that "we all need to come together to protest the mayor's foolish spending habits that brought New York City to bankruptcy"! is a narrative. If you can keep interrupting their outcries, then you slowed their roll. (Like I mentioned ala the victories bit.) If you can explicitly state where they aren't dealing with reality, but only a story based on someone's else's opinions, then you are taking away the tracks for their rage choo choo. Dramatic stories act like a trance state. An old saying used to be that analyzing a dream (or a nightmare) kills it.

Short-cicuit the drama

Humans run on emotions. Some make a habit of trying to feel certain ones. Cry Bullies are drama junkies. They have to keep getting that fix. Witch Hunts are swarms of people attempting to get and keep their outrage-high. Instead of promptly responding with heated denials, use their own stereotypes aginst them. Instead of saying something like "I would never do that! That's just evil!" pick one of the rainclouds in the Witch Hunt, act like a proper mansplainer, and say something like: "Unfortunately, you're wrong, and you seem quite emotional. One of your mistakes is that you used your opinions to build your case, instead of verified facts..." This will "trigger" them, and they will likely either shriek at you, or they will try to shut you down by using gas-lighting tactics. Call them on that. If they shriek, keep pointing out to the group that the other person seems very upset over their personal issues, and perhaps needs to speak to someone, but you deny their charges. Then state something like: "I feel this matter should be dropped, unless the raincloud wants to show some proof. Let's get back to..." If the Cry Bully instead tries to use gas-lighting tactics, you should pointout to the group each time it happens. Ask group memebers if they approve of boundary violations such as accusing other people without evidence. Then say something like: "Let's drop this here and now, unless ..." and go back to what you were doing. (If the raincloud keeps gathering up people to build a Witch Hunt, you might want to talk to a lawyer, or at least Legal Aid.)

Undermine the judge

The culture or group you're in points out who you consider "smart" or "wise" or "has a lot of good common sense." That's a form of social credit - some cultures call it "respect." A Witch Hunt needs to that smart/wise/common-sense person buy into the Witch Hunt. If they can't get that respected group member, then the Witch Hunt can't make the jump from being a splinter group issue to an issue for the whole group. If the Hunters lose that Judge, then they need to find another one. So what makes a Judge? A Judge shows the traits that a group values, and shows that "common sense." Working to disable the Judge brings up a problem: Will you only work to get the Judge to leave the Hunt, or will you also discredit the Judge? Will you work to make the Judge look foolish? Will you work to make the Judge look less than honorable? That's a trap. If you go and attack the Judge, the other Hunters can try to make you again look like a bad guy.

If you can, try to get the Judge to just leave the Hunt. Ask the would be Judge how they know the accusations are true. Not just "the Hunters have a good or fun argument, and I think I can go along" but TRUE. Can they prove it with facts? Would the Judge want the same level of "proof" used against them? Ask what price is the Judge willing to pay, when they find out they are wrong? How will the Judge being wrong hurt the rest of the group? Why are the Witch Hunters trying to hurt the group? Ask these quesitons. Try to have some answers that show YOU are a good guy that helps keep the background group together. If you can't get the Judge onboard, you have to make them look less useful to the larger group. Point out the Judge's factual and logical mistakes. Either way, there's going to be bad feelings. Decide if that concerns you, suck it up, and move on. You will need to listen carefully to what the Judge says, and then quickly point out the mistakes.

Dropping the hammer

Getting outside groups involved always involves at least some bad feelings. Getting legal authorities involved means a group's informal style is going to get examined. Getting legal authorities involved can also be tough. Why would police want to be involved in a subculture? Did someone get hurt, or break the law? If so, police can get interested. Did someone get fired illegally? Lawyers can get involved. Make the Cry Bullies spell out each and every fact to an outside authority. Find a good lawyer and start going over plans. But before you drop that call in lawyers, reach to whoever runs that group. Before you call in the heavies, walk through the following steps: *No-stop-go away-tell.* Most groups, companies, or institutions have a rule that says that if someone says a version of those words, your non business or legal interactions with them are done. Learn that rule and use it. If your conversation is interrupted or disrupted by a Cry Bully or any flavor (raincloud up to full witch hunt), turn and say – especially publicly – to them "No, I do not want to talk with you. Stop talking to me. Go away from me." Then move 20 feet away from them (that's about seven or so long paces). If they walk over to you, tell the local authority that said raincloud is harassing you, and you wish to file a complaint/charges. By the group's rules, the other person is a harasser, and said person now faces whatever penalties the group dishes out. Taking this action is going hardcore, and one of you is probably leaving. If the group decides to support the raincloud, it's better that you leave anyway.

At the certain point, the rainclouds will pitch a fit about other people not doing their bidding. Some rainclouds may try to stop you, when you defend yourself against their games. Recognize that rainclouds consider *your* counterattacks to be unprovoked attacks. If you defend yourself, you will likely be seen as an attacker. Your choices are walk away, spin some threads of good PR, or embrace the suck. Each of their "defenses" to your counterattacks can show their own "styles" or "tone" - if you want get snarky and "use the language of the oppressor." The commonest macro-style of response to the raincloud's attack ("hey raincloud, you are being nasty") can be summed up by the acronym DARVO: *Deny Attack – Reverse Victim/Offender*. (Jennifer Freyd talked about this in her article "Violations of power, adaptive blindness, and betrayal trauma theory" in *Feminism & Psychology*. While she and that magazine definitely have a dog in the fight, the idea is worth looking at.) If one has the audacity to actually counter or otherwise fight back, that's when the rainclouds use DARVO. In the *Deny Attack* phase, said raincloud is gonna try to show a sliding process of "it didn't happen, but if it did, then the other party deserved it." Look for a crowd – or maybe a better way to phrase it is the Cry Bullies play to "the crowd." One reason is to get more people on the raincloud's "side." Also, the raincloud's words are a way to show they are down with the cause/struggle. Another reason is to remove those people the rainclouds consider obstacles. Rainclouds often don't really see *People*, as much as they see members of groups/collectives.

The next step is *Reverse Victim Offender*. Good reader,

please remember that no one has the right to make you a victim. No one has the right to use emotional blackmail and/or make you a slave to their whim. If someone comes up to you and starts demanding that you repent for some alleged sin, based on a trait you share with a large group...You have the right to walk away. Walking away means that the basic and immediate parts of DARVO stop, and all of the next 8 large scale strategies lose a whole lot of their power. Almost all of the dynamic of DARVO is built around you continuing to respond, or to switch positions in the minds of the bystanders. In order to create this switch, the rainclouds will usually use one of eight techniques. (Said rainclouds often use these to shut down dissent against their agenda. Watch for them, adjust your efforts, and keep nailing down your points.)

Fallacy Checklist

In 1831, there was a guy named Arthur Schopenhauer, who had worked out a list of the 38 argumentative tricks he'd seen/read/heard to "win over" crowds during debates. (Hey, don't judge too harshly. They had few forms of cheap and string-free fun back then...) Schopenhauer wrote it all up in a book called "The Art of Being Right." Looking over the collected piles of drama wars in Academia, and other walks of life, I've noticed that that list of 38 arguments could be whittled down by a lot. Most of the raincloud counter-arguments run to a quick list of 10 attack styles: *Stretch, Twist, Ignore, Anger, Concede to Fog, Throw-away point, Obstacle, Push A Small Flaw, Interrupt,* and *Widen The Focus.* Some seem like just shadings of others, but the end-effects can be different.

STRETCH opposing arguments beyond their natural limits; exaggerate all of your opponent's positions. The looser the statement, the harder to defend it. Let the raincloud make the hazy and windy statements. Make sure your own arguments are wired tight. Keep your facts simple and relevant. Keep your arguments to only a handful of consistent statements. The more general your statement becomes, the more objections the raincloud can find against your whole argument. Tight lists of facts and propositions are easier defend. If the raincloud can get away with STRETCHing your positions, the raincloud may move on to the next form, TWISTING arguments.

TWIST your opponent's words to refute or ignore his argument. Often, the raincloud is going to go for a hot button. If you are at a convention, concert, party, or mall, and a raincloud shows up to start an on-the-fly talk about their favorite issue, common courtesy would suggest that politely asking the raincloud to avoid interfering with the games in play would be appropriate. The raincloud can TWIST your request into a script for "dominant groups suppressing important conversations about" and they'll name their cause. If someone tries this one you, a quick and easy way to deal with it, is to say a simple "That's not what I meant. I feel you just tried to twist my words. I was talking about..." and then go back to your points.

IGNORE your opponent's statements and/context. The raincloud will likely act like your statement pointed to some particular thing, and not at all what you meant – this one works nicely with the TWIST trick. They will purposefully misunderstand your words - and then refute *that*. Basically, they will attack something different than what you said. For those playing the home game, this is the classic "Straw Man" fallacy (as described eariler). You can always the use the classic "Are you having some other argument? Your replies just don't make sense, regarding what I've been talking about."

ANGER your opponent. Angry people lose a bunch of their judgment/skills, and rapidly go tunnel vision on a given target. Don't be a bull, or fooled by the same. Again, rule zero for dealing with a lot of rainclouds is "Don't lose your cool." (Easy to say, hard to do. Practice ahead of time...) A quick way to piss off a raincloud – while maybe hitting the mental pause button – is to yawn at them. Yawning is a display (at least in us humans) that shows you are bored with the speaker. Also, when you yawn (the kind that makes that comedy YA-AA-W-W-N) the "hum" blocks out a lot of sound. Kind of makes it makes it hard to take the raincloud seriously, doesn't it? Your yawn doesn't have to be very loud. It just has to be loud enough to damp out the "interior" sound of the raincloud.

When you refute all of the raincloud's points, the raincloud may try to get you to agree to a minor or THROW-AWAY point, and then seem to reverse some part of their argument. This is supposed to confuse you about the raincloud's goals, and maybe get you to reverse your argument. Think of the old Bug Bunny and Daffy Duck routine "Rabbit Season, Duck Season." (If you don't get that, go search the net, watch the clip, and then come back. I'll wait....) This is another Fogging type of attack, and a lot of people will most likely say "it'll never happen to me" - but people often fall for it. When you're tired, or stressed, or pushed for time, any win sounds good. It'll sound like a good idea, just to agree with the raincloud. Watch out when you are tired. Sometimes, it helps to call out the raincloud: "You know, you were just pushing the opposite point a minute ago. Is there some reason? Are you suddenly agreeing with me, or are you playing Rabbit season/Duck season?" Then go back to your point. Act like a broken record.

When you state a goal or action, the raincloud can go for building an OBSTACLE. They will ask a question that questions your commitment to your cause/argument. For example: if you defend somebody's "right" to die, the raincloud will likely ask

"Why don't you go kill yourself?" If you dislike something about the city you live in, the raincloud could pipe in with, "Why don't you leave on the first plane?" Good reader, you will see this style of argument used to interrupt your "flow" of speech. Once you've mentioned one or two statements that suggest action, they'll pop up with a direct statement. They're looking to see you contradict yourself. If you are for enforced deportation of undocumented inhabitants in the United States, they'll ask when are you leaving? For Gay Marriage? When are you getting married? Here's a counter question: Why does a supporter of a position need to be directly tied to that position? Do you have to be Native American, in order to defend Native American rights? You can call out the raincloud: "I'm also against animal abuse. Do I look like a llama?" Point this out to the raincloud, and then continue your argument.

If you ask the raincloud for counter-proof, the raincloud can sometimes PUSH A SMALL FLAW in your argument. They will try to find a second meaning or a way to make your ideas sound/seem ambiguous. This is another version of a twisting argument.

The rainclouds will INTERRUPT arguments that wreck their side. The raincloud won't allow you to carry those arguments to their conclusion. They'll try to Interrupt your arguments, points, or facts. Again: keep nailing your points down.

Keep your calm and keep speaking. They'll even sometimes just walk away from a set of your positions – seemingly tuning into new subjects. This gets into another of those interruption arguments.

If you challenge the raincloud to prove you wrong, and the raincloud lacks facts, they can try to WIDEN THE FOCUS, and make their nay saying less specific. As you might have guessed, this is another version of fogging. Unless you are willing to nail down your points, and theirs, you could find yourself following a Will o' the Wisp, deeper and deeper into the swamps. As they say, *don't go there...* As before, so again: keep your arguments wired tight. When they try to widen the focus, narrow your statements back in to your original points. They may try to de-rail your getting back to your arguments with something like "why are you repeating yourself?" If they do, ask why they were trying to fog the issue, restate your points, and keep going.

All of these techniques are used to distract an opponent, or to get you to tangle yourself up in your own words. If you feel you have to respond, you can now politely point out when someone uses such chicanery. But remember, you have the right to get out of the rain. There are very few events where you actually HAVE TO listen to a raincloud's complaint. It may help keep things smooth at work, but you – usually – don't have to listen. If you know the raincloud is wrong, you can just listen, nod, and then go back to whatever you were doing. Or, you can give them a friendly "No, thank you," and get back to doing your own thing.

Arise – This is the toughie. Ask yourself a few questions: What do you want from the group that's having the fight. Can they provide those things? Are getting those things worth dealing with the rainclouds? Can you answer yes to each questions? No? Then maybe it's time to leave. If the people running the party are hooked in with the cry bullies, then there's not much hope for that party. Sometimes, it's best to leave, and warn the others. It's easier to leave a group, if you don't need a particular job (instead of "a job"), or you don't need to get a degree from a particular school, or you have other "good" people to hang out with. If you think that you could lose your job, contact an attorney, or legal aid. Document every situation that the cry bullies and your chain of bosses act on. If you have advance warning, then try to quietly check out other jobs, perhaps in a city where there are fewer cry bullies. Take your time at checking things out. Very few schools have a monopoly on degrees. There are certain schools where getting a degree from them bumps you up the employment list, but only for a few subjects - Subjects like literature, certain areas of history, and philosophy. Do you NEED to get a degree from that particular institution? Is it worth the "price" of dealing with a pack of entrenched Cry Bullies? Spend a few weeks looking into different ways to get the training, certification, and permits that you need to further yourself.

Short Circuiting Alinsky's Rules

There are ethical, social, and practical considerations about counter-attacking. Every society has rules that members don't break without a cost. If someone is willing to break those rules, it means there's a good chance that the breaker/raincloud has other problems in their mix. Most people try to avoid making waves. Someone feeling mad enough to make waves means that they are upset/hurting. While you don't have to be somebody's punching bag, it can be a bad thing to curb stomp an emotional cripple.

Societies create a (supposedly) shared view of what is "good." Many times, the "right thing to do" involves how to keep their group/tribe/nation running smoothly for as long as possible. Members of a society act on this view – this can be called an "ethos." Rainclouds are usually trying to change the group's rules, while staying protected by that group. When you can take the attacker away from the cover of acceptable behavior, they lose a lot of their power. Point out how the raincloud is hurting the group, in a way that said group can understand, and that group will very likely start looking at the raincloud in a new light – you might be able to shake the automatic acceptance of the raincloud's "narrative." By pointing out a danger to the group in question, there is an opportunity to "switch the witch," should you deem that necessary…

Most of the tricks that the rainclouds use follow those sets of tactics/tools that I've talked about. They follow in a rough collection of steps in "rules." When an opponent writes up a list of rules how they operate, use it against them. Say what you want about Alinsky…. His 13 rules work. A quick read through these rules suggests that they are used by rainclouds, to keep their own energy going. If they stop using these rules, or these rules get disrupted, these rainclouds fade away.

Alinsky's 13 rules are:

Power is not only what you have, but what the enemy thinks you have." Power is derived from 2 main sources – money and people. *"Have-Nots" must build power from flesh and blood."* (Alinsky, Rules for Radicals, pg. 127.)

"Never go outside the expertise of your people." It results in confusion, fear and retreat. Feeling secure adds to the backbone of anyone. (Alinsky, pg. 127.)

"Whenever possible, go outside the expertise of the enemy." Look for ways to increase insecurity, anxiety and uncertainty. (Alinsky, pg. 127.)

"Make the enemy live up to its own book of rules." (Alinsky, pg. 128.)

"Ridicule is man's most potent weapon." (Alinsky, pg. 128.)

"A good tactic is one your people enjoy." (Alinsky, pg. 128)

"A tactic that drags on too long becomes a drag." (Alinsky, pg. 128.)

"Keep the pressure on. Never let up." (Alinsky, pg. 128.)

"The threat is usually more terrifying than the thing itself." (Alinsky, pg. 129.)

"The major premise for tactics is the development of operations that will maintain a constant pressure upon the opposition." (Alinsky, pg. 129.)

"If you push a negative hard enough, it will break through into its counterside." (Alinsky, pg. 129.)

"The price of a successful attack is a constructive alternative." (Alinsky, pg. 130.)

"Pick the target, freeze it, personalize it, and polarize it." (Alinsky, pg. 130.)

"Power is not only what you have, but what the enemy thinks you have." Power is derived from 2 main sources – money and people. "Have-Nots" must build power from flesh

and blood." (Alinsky, Rules for Radicals, pg. 127.) Rainclouds need to have more organization and numbers than their target. This gives away the fact that many of the rainclouds are bullies. Their actions are intended to show power over others. If you keep *not* acquiescing, then the rainclouds loss that sense of rolling victories. They need that string of "virtuous victories" to keep the head of steam going. They will try to amp up the pressure to make you fall at something... but that either fades away, or meets the hard deck realities of the real world and the real life court rooms. (There's an old saying from one corner of the gaming world: "Everybody's a bad ass until the shotguns or the lawyers show up.") On a deeper level, this shows a "reason" for the raincloud's bad behavior. They feel they have nothing to offer, and that they must take from others. Not trade – take – as in to steal. They'll most likely try to shift the blame onto you. Don't buy in to it. Remember, no one has the right to abuse you, or steal from you. There is no "right" that says the rainclouds get to gang up on you. Matter of fact, doing so could be illegal – check with your local laws and a good attorney.

EXERCISE:

1.) Write down ten ideas that you think are important.

2.) rewrite those ideas so that they start with phrases like "I feel that."

3.) rewrite those ideas so that they sound like an accusing

fact. "Isn't it true that..."

4.) rewrite them so that they sound like a group belief: "We feel that..."

5.) rewrite them so that they sound like you are emotionally distancing yourself from it "I can see that you feel that..."

6.) Ask a friend to give you ten "I like" phrases.

7.) rewrite your friend's phrases with the emotional distance style, like in step 5.

__"Never go outside the expertise of your people." It results in confusion, fear and retreat. Feeling secure adds to the backbone of anyone.__ (Alinsky, Rules for Radicals, pg. 127.) If you can, find out what skill sets the rainclouds use/have. Then find out where they show the gaps in their arguments, skill set, or what have you. The easiest way to use this one is to use that full Jesuit mode. When they make a mistake, call them on it – and back up your answers with training/skills that they don't have. If they cry out that you are derailing them, point out that derailing a train that's bound for the cliff is a public service. This tactic – and the following tactic – show opposite sides of an important coin: he who controls the narrative, controls the "conversation." (With apologies to Frank Herbert…)

EXERCISE:

1.) Ask someone to explain something, without their favorite place holder phrase ("like" "you know" "let me put it this way." and the like.) When you hear your friend using a placeholder word, tell them to stop, and say the sentence again, but without the place holder word.

2.) Have someone explain how to tie a shoe, verbally.

3.) Ask someone to recite a phone number, and then ask someone to read a phone number from a piece of paper

4.) Look for the shift in behaviors between parts one, two, and three. That shift is the difference between some thinking on the fly, and simply reciting a set of words or actions. When you find that shift in a person's conversation, you have found a weak point.

__"Whenever possible, go outside the expertise of the enemy." Look for ways to increase insecurity, anxiety and uncertainty.__ (Alinsky, Rules for Radicals, pg. 127.) If you decide to dive into the study the rainclouds culture, you've got a better than average shot of noticing many of the writings are about pissing people off. They want to make others feel growing doubt about resisting the raincloud. To some eyes, these kinds of tactics can seem abusive and predatory. (Gee, I wonder what groups actively use insecurity and anxiety to force someone to do something against their will, for the pleasures of said predator?)

Remember that kind of thing when a raincloud tries to butt into a conversation with stuff out of left field, and then starts up with stuff that seems designed to make you uncomfortable. This point is where they drag in their "experts," and try to deflect your facts and logic. Specifically ask them what is the purpose of bringing up irrelevant material. "Going Jesuit" works pretty well against this one.

This also works when dealing with a person in the "Judge" role. A quick defense against a judge is calling them out as a Greek chorus or back-up singers. Other quick tricks include sticking to hard facts, and error-checking the 'studies' that the Judge uses. If the 'studies' are flawed, then the Judge looks bad. If the Judge looks bad, then it's a pretty quick trip to take down the oppressed raincloud. If the source of their "expertise" goes down, the raincloud loses their vehicle's power.

EXERCISE:

1.) Interrupt the Cry Bully in mid speech, when they are trying to cite an "authority's" speech. Ask how did that person become an authority?

2.) Then ask them to quote some piece, without their placeholder words, or buzzwords.

3.) Then ask what emotional connection they have to the authority.

4.) Then ask for the statement that the Judge said before

they brought up the author.

5.) Each time they say something, ask the full background.

6.) Mix up the order of the questions.

"Make the enemy live up to its own book of rules."

(Alinsky, Rules for Radicals, pg. 128.) Two ways to go on this rule. You can ignore them actively (AKA telling them to butt out), and the more active path. Two pieces to the more active fork: 1. Examine your own rules, and remove flawed rules and structures (AKA: keep your rules wired tight). 2. Listen to and use the raincloud's own rule-flaws. The rainclouds talk about justice and equity a lot. So be it. Unless they are trying to propose and force a hidden double standard, then I'm sure they would impartially mete out equal sentences for a crime – regardless of race, gender, class, etc. I'm sure the rainclouds would **never** stoop to pushing unfair practices. What would the public think if the rainclouds kept getting caught out in unfair behavior? I'm shocked! Shocked, I tell you! (Let me put the safety back on my sarcasm…)

EXERCISE:

1.) List five ways that a potential opponent attacks targets.

2.) List the phrases they might use.

3.) List the noble goals they mention.

4.) List how their actions would actually be going against

their goals.

"Ridicule is man's most potent weapon." (Alinsky, Rules for Radicals, pg. 128.) A great counter to someone trying to use ridicule, is to use the same technique right back – just add more humor. When someone tries to use ridicule, do something like calling out "Hey everybody, so and so is trying to use the ridicule technique! Let's give them a big hand for trying so hard!" Then, when they try another social mugging attempt, find your inner child and tell the raincloud just how "aah-DOR-able" they are, or how their next sentence "was a really good try." Another way to counter the ridicule game: when the rainclouds use sarcasm, it shows they feel they need to be "pushy." That suggests they feel pressed for time. Drag it out. If you have stopped feeling charitable, then start picking away at their structure. As the raincloud why their comment is funny. When they ask if you "can't take a joke," point out that your sense of humor is just fine, thank you, and how exactly is their joke "supposed to be funny?" Keep on pressing them for details. Keep asking exactly how their "joke" is related to your original conversation. Again, at counter attack to this "rule" is to keep hammering away at your opponent.

EXERCISE:

1.) Look at any existing "humor" that a likely attacker would use.

2.) Look at any "jokes" that go for a cheap laugh. (The Cry Bullies will bring up sex pretty quick).

3.) Write down three ways to over-examine the "jokes" you found. (Example: "Why do you think that joke should be funny?" "Is there a reason you think the joke should be funny?)

4.) Go back to your conversation.

"A good tactic is one your people enjoy." (Alinsky, Rules for Radicals, pg. 128) People do things to either avoid pain, attain pleasure, or seek connections. Make the social mugging more and more costly, and the rainclouds will drift away. Expect some noise and turbulence, but remember – the rainclouds *have to* keep scoring easy victories. The more you make that "victory" cost, the more followers the raincloud will lose. Much earlier, I mentioned the concept of the Three Wheeled Clown Car. The wheels of the car are Catchiness, Drama, and Triumph. A simple way of blowing up the Catchiness aspect is to start out with "where did you hear that?" If the person can't answer, or won't answer, then it's pretty simple to ask them if they'd believe unfounded rumors, or you can say you simply won't answer to smear campaigns. (To really get edgy, you can ask why the speaker likes slinging slander around…) One way to blow up the Drama wheel is to use the "yes and…" technique. Most Drama is built on the idea of immediate negation by the accused side. So, instead, you can take their accusation and run with it! "You heard that I hit him? Worse, I dropped an elephant on him. Really bad for the elephant – it stubbed its trunk." To pop the Triumph wheel, you need to make playing games cost more than the rainclouds are willing to pay. Most people have a limit on how long they are willing to keep wasting energy on a task that doesn't get them something. If you can keep making them spend their energy, and don't give them the "wins" they feel they need, they will eventually give up and leave. The question becomes when. The important thing is to keep de-coupling/destroying any sense of momentum the raincloud seems to be building. The slower and shorter their roll, the less damage the raincloud can do when they hit something. If a tactic keeps losing more energy than it gains them, the rainclouds will likely shift tactics and "rules." This leads to the next "rule"...

EXERCISE:

1.) Look up vidoes online that show protesters actions, reactions, and facial gestures.

2.) Look at which action/reaction sets invoke protester interest.

3.) write down three ways that you could short circuit that set of actions.

4.) Write down the pieces for those short circuits.

5.) When you see a similar tactic, stretch out the short circuit pieces.

"A tactic that drags on too long becomes a drag."

(Alinsky, Rules for Radicals, pg. 128.) Make the raincloud backtrack and prove every single point in their rant. When they start in with "derailing," point out the logical fallacies they use, the steps in propaganda thinking they show, etc. Do what you can to maintain your own calm. Also – if you can – keep talking during their rant. The rainclouds like to talk while others are talking, to try and drown out the messages that the rainclouds don't like. Turn-about is fair play... Why should you have to be quiet and listen to them rant? The minute they begin speaking, just yawn and talk about your points. Every time they talk, you talk. Take out a book and loudly and humorously start reading from it. (May I suggest passages from the deeper erotic mysteries of the IRS Schedule C Instructions?)

EXERCISE:

1.) Point out a tactic that the Crybully has used. When they deny that they've used that tactic, quote their post/thread/email/speech that shows they've used that tactic.

2.) When the Raincloud tries to "move on" from discussing the tactic, ask the raincloud why they don't want to discuss the raincloud's actions/speech? Ask if there's a reason they feel ashamed of the tactic.

3.) When they try to get you to drop the matter, ask them if they feel some sort of "need" to use those tactics.

*"**Keep the pressure on. Never let up.**"* (Alinsky, Rules for Radicals, pg. 128.) Pressure means someone is using up energy. People and groups have only so much energy to use. Many rainclouds show emotional problems, and a shrewd man could have one or two friends that keep using up the raincloud's drama/energy. Interrupting an interrupter sounds fair to me – and maybe a form of instant karma. Another move is to keep turning away from the rainclouds, breaking up your groups into smaller units to move through crowds, and then reforming away from the rainclouds. Who is the pursuer here? The general public doesn't like people that chase after others to yell at them over made up grudges. Unless the other guy is pointing a weapon at you, you can win by outlasting the bastard. If an attacker uses up more energy than the defender does, then the attacker is on a timetable. You win, if you are still standing when they run out of time or energy. Don't be where he swings, and don't let yourself get cornered.

EXERCISE:

1.) Write down a typical raincloud post.

2.) Break down the post sentence by sentence, or "idea by idea."

3.) Give a response for each sentence of idea. Avoid all "hot button" words in your responses.

4.) Build a summary statement after you have responded to each idea.

__"The threat is usually more terrifying than the thing itself."__ (Alinsky, Rules for Radicals, pg. 129.)

The most direct way to deal with this is to immediately call them out on threats. Ask them, point blank: "Is that a threat? Are you threatening me with assault and battery?" If they are blocking all of your travel routes, tell them: "I can't move forward (into the building, out of the building, etc). You are stopping me from leaving. Please move aside, and stop detaining me." If/when they insist that you stay put, tell them "You are holding me against my will. That is a crime." If they refuse to let you into a building for legally approved business, mention that restraint of trade is also a crime. Then call the cops on them. Many states made it a felony to try to intimidate someone from speaking. That's right...videos showing the rainclouds trying to silence people via the rainclouds yelling/threatening may be evidence of a felony – again, check your local laws and a good attorney. Either way, when you point out that their threats have real world consequences, you force them to consider their commitment to "The Cause."

EXERCISE:

1.) Look up the Assault and Battery, Breach of Peace, and Self Defense laws in your state.

2.) Look up the public recording laws in your state. If allowed, wear a personal body camera.

3.) Write up a set of questions to ask the intimidator about making threat (make sure your body cam can hear those quesitons.)

"The major premise for tactics is the development of operations that will maintain a constant pressure upon the opposition." (Alinsky, Rules for Radicals, pg. 129.) Dig it. They need to make those attacks to build a culture. They need to keep attacking, and they need a running string of wins. At the same time, they NEED for the background public to see the poor rainclouds being attacked by those evil mean fill-in-the-blanks.

EXERCISE:

1.) Watch videos that show the larger sit-ins and protests.

2.) Look at the messages on the signs.

3.) How many of those signs just show messages with funny themes? a sign just aying "I don't like this" is a funny type of sign.)

4.) How many of those signs are protesting something? (A great example from the sixties would be the old "Impeach Nixon" signs.

5.) How many of those signs sign show a message of needing to unite against an evil thing? (Example: "Socialists against Bernie Sanders."

6.) Watch which signholders stand with which other signholders.

7.) Watch the videos again. Look at who starts the violence.

8.) Write down five ways to short circuit the sign that shows the group identity. Shutting that protest message slows down the "build and maintain constant pressure" tactic.

"If you push a negative hard enough, it will break through into its counterside." (Alinsky, Rules for Radicals, pg. 129.) Alinsky used the term "counterside." Most dictionaries don't cover this word, so one could easily state the term is a form of word fogging. A better way to describe this is "lemons into lemonade." If they are talking about their oppression, and you start mentioning real oppression (like African starvation rates), they will kijely say that you are trying to silence them. This one can get hard, as the rainclouds usually try to tap into the public sympathy well before they really start it up. The best way to defuse this one is to keep rephrasing their statements…Make them rephrase each one. Whenever they try to paint you as a villain and them being the valiant oppressed person fighting back, break each piece down, and point out they are being abusive.

EXERCISE:

1.) Find and read through five sets of internet messages regarding Oppression.

2.) Look for the person that starts out with how Oppressed they are.

3.) Look at who responds with more apparent actual Oppression, and how they mention questions of scale.

4) Look for the switching point when the Cry Bully claims that the other people are trying to create a "contest," and therefore ignore the cries of the Cry Bully.

5.) Write down which pieces of the tactic that you could find.

6.) Write down five uses of Nailing your points down, and five uses of Going Jesuit, used against those switching point pieces.

__"The price of a successful attack is a constructive alternative."__ (Alinsky, Rules for Radicals, pg. 130.) Show why the raincloud's solutions won't work, before they can bring it up.

If you can, rattle off their solutions, and the flaws each one has, in one long breath. Otherwise, keep speaking at your normal speaking pace, interrupting them as needed. If YOU can bring up workable solutions faster than they can, they look silly. Remember, most rainclouds don't have much to offer groups they want to invade/infect. Taking away steps from Monroe's sequence takes away their working tools, leaving them with only "I don't like this" complaints - and that makes them look like whining brats.

EXERCISE:

1.) Spend some time looking at videos of cry bullies.

2.) Try to match their attack forms with their clothing and ornaments.

3.) Write down the solutions mentioned in the videos.

4.) Write down logical points why those solutions won't work

5. Write down five phrases showing you are going back to your conversation and shutting out the cry bully.

__"Pick the target, freeze it, personalize it, and polarize it."__
(Alinsky, Rules for Radicals, pg. 130.)

As mentioned earlier, one point of these attacks is to keep up morale. Emotions will be high. The more you blur their presentation of you, the more confusing a target you become. On the other side of that coin… If you can flip the script of your attacker, they start looking like the predatory assholes that they are. Most groups **really** don't like it when someone acts like a bully. This is why the bullies keep trying to "other" their targets – as per this Alinsky rule. Point out the tactic, and the raincloud in question then has to cover up that fact. Most people don't like it when someone is trying to trick them into witch hunting. Point out how much witch hunting looks a LOT like racism. The raincloud wouldn't actually be a racist, would they? Bring up fogging tactics, when you see them used. Would the raincloud be trying to blur things and avoid logic? The raincloud wouldn't be using those tactics to bully someone into silence, would they? Would the raincloud actually be using abusive tactics, just like someone who beats their wife? The point that Alinsky was making was that the rainclouds should go after "easy" targets. Make yourself a non other-able person, and the raincloud has a much tougher job.

Short circuiting the background "rules" of abusive people makes them a lot more visible. Without cover, it's very hard for a raincloud to go for cheap shots. Every loss these characters rack up slows their role. Rainclouds thrive on handing out abuse – If nothing else, you don't have to let them make you their next victim of abuse.

EXERCISE:

1.) Find five videos of Cry Bullies protesting something.

2.) Write down the steps the Cry Bullies take, to focus their protesting on a small group of people who object to the protest.

3.) Listen to the language used by the swarming protesters.

4.) Pick one of those five videos.

5.) Write down the parts of the protester's speech that focus on provocative language. (Example: "You sound like a bigot!" "You need to shut up and listen!" "You aren't welcome here!"

6) Pick a provocative statement, break it down into pieces, and compare it to Monroe's Sequence. Then see if the statement shows an attempt to put the Cry Bully in the hero beating evil (said evil guy being the one arguing against the Cry Bully.)

7.) Write replies to the Cry Bully's attacking phrase. (Example: If the video states something like "Trying to stay neutral is siding with the Oppressor!" Write a reply asking them if they understand the term "Non-combatant". Example: If the video shows the Cry Bully starting their attack phrase with "You always," write a reply that rephrases everything in E-prime.

Afterword

I've talked about why the rainclouds attack, and the rhetoric they use to build those attacks. The ways they try to distract from the fact that they ARE attacking, shows that they know (at some level) that most people don't like bullies – crying or not. These tricks and insults created massive wavefronts of division and hostility that have – and continue to – sweep throughout our country. Some of these waves track back to the 1930's. It surfaces again in the 1960's. Your personal perspective will steer your call on if you see the Cry Bullies as a conspiracy or as an emergent behavior. Given all that, just knowing that there are ways to fight back against the Cry Bullies can give the reader hope. The tips and techniques in this book can help you take that hope and direct a fan against the Cry Bullies' self puffing rainclouds.

Wandering into a script. Take Two:

You, talking to friends: "Chicago's crime scene is getting completely out of hand."

SJW: "That's Racist!"

You: "I'm not talking about race, I'm talking about safety. Why are you trying to hijack our conversation?"

SJW: "You are being problematic about a very large community of People Of Color!"

You: "You seem to be under the impression that we have to talk to you. We don't have to."

SJW, interrupting: "DO YOU HAVE **ANY** IDEA WHAT YOU SOUND LIKE?

You: "No one cares…"

SJW: "Have you no EMPATHY?"

You: "Is that gaslighting?"

SJW: "So you condone institutionalized racism…"

You: "Shame on you for trying to strawman an argument."

SJW: "OH! MY! GOD! Can you be ANY more SEXIST? **MANSPLAINING** LIKE THAT!?"

You: "You seem to have your own script. Why should I be a part of it?"

SJW: "WHY ARE YOU IGNORING MY *FEELINGS*?

You: "The rug sings to us of sweet gothic erotic tax returns…"

SJW: "WHAT???"

You: "We don't want to talk to you. Stop talking to us. Go away, or it's police complaint time."

Bob Juliano taught people with special needs, "normal" people, and a few gifted folks. He started writing after watching the same drama games played in Academia, then in science fiction fandom, and finally in "normal" life. Besides writing, he enjoys flying, building things as the mood strikes him, and old school gaming.

Bibliography

Part One

"Return to camp suicide: 30 years on, could the nightmare of Jonestown happen again?," By David Jones. *Daily Mail.* Http://www.dailymail.co.uk/news/article-1085869/Return-camp-suicide-30-years- nightmare-Jonestown-happen-again.html#ixzz4WkI6lCpp

Antonio Gramsci, try the Oxford Research Encyclopedia: http://communication.oxfordre.com/view/10.1093/acrefor e/9780190228613.001.0001/ acrefore-9780190228613-e-78 (You may have to put and paste two pieces for this one...)

To Be or Not: An E-Prime Anthology, by Bourland, D. David; Johnston, Paul Dennithorne.(1991)

"Culture and Cognitive Science" S*tanford Encyclopedia of Philosophy,* https://plato.stanford.edu/entries/culture-cogsci/ *The Rise of Political Correctness,* by Angelo Codevilla Angelo. (2016)

Rules for Radicals by Saul Alinsky

(http://www.claremont.org/download_pdf.php?file_name=
1106 1989).

The-racefail-09-flamewar-timeline.html, Do Not Engage by Will
Shetterly (2012)
http://shetterly.blogspot.com/2012/09/the-racefail-09-flamewar-
timeline.html

*How to make a Social Justice Warrior: On identitarianism,
intersectionality, mobbing, racefail, and failfans 2005-
2014* by Will Shetterly (2014).

Part Two

"Man's enemies are not demons, but human beings like himself,"
a saying attributed to Lao Tzu (D. 531 BC)

"The feminist freakout over the scientist's 'girly' shirt," by Jonah
Goldberg, *L A Times.*
Http://www.latimes.com/opinion/op-ed/la-oe-goldberg-
rosetta-scientist-shirtgate- feminists-
20141118column.html.

Nail 'Em! Confronting High-Profile Attacks on Celebrities and Businesses, by Eric Dezenhall.(2003).

For the Uninitiated: Social Justice Warrior, by EyeisBloke (2016).
https://eyeisbloke.com/2016/08/31/for-the-uninitiated-social-justice-warrior/

Why I don't like Social Justice Warriors, By Larry Correia. (2014).
http://monsterhunternation.com/2014/11/14/why-I-dont-like-social-justice-warriors/

Part Three

Fountains of faith;: The words of William Arthur Ward, by William Arthur Ward, (1970).

"Performative Acts and Gender Constitution: An Essay In Phenomenology And Feminist Theory," by Judith Butler. *The Feminist Philosophy Reader* (2008).
https://sites.sas.upenn.edu/educationglobal/files/the_feminist_philosophy_reader_-_alison_bailey.pdf

"Postmodernism Disrobed" in *Nature*, 9 July 1998, vol. 394, pp. 141-143.

http://www.physics.nyu.edu/faculty/sokal/dawkins.html

Negative Dialectics, by Theodor Adorno, (2003)

The Essential Frankfurt School Reader, by Arato, Andrew; Eike Gephart, eds. (1982).

Lord Of The Rings, by J. R. R. Tolkien (1954).

Tribes by Steve Jackson Games. (2015)
http://www.sjgames.com/tribes/

"Nomic" by Hofstadter, Douglas. *Metamagical Themas: Questing for the Essence of Mind and Pattern* (1996).

Robert's Rules of Order by General Henry M. Robert, (1876).

Monroe's Motivated Sequence by A. H. Monroe (1943).

"The 69 non material needs," *The Book of Visions: Encyclopaedia of Social Innovations.*
By Nicholas Albery (Editor) (1992).

The Art of Being Right by Arthur Schopenhauer (2015).

Appendix

Sanctuaries

Write this on a piece of paper: *there is more than one game in town.* Just about any culture you can name has gotten so large that no one group can take over all the pieces on the table. The internet is a system that short circuits "last life boat" thinking. Instead, ask yourself "is this the right group for me..." Skip worrying about getting tossed out of "the only group I know," and build a better plan. Meet and defend like minded people, and bring the battle to the opponent. Building sanctuaries means you are focused on solutions instead of conflicts. Join or create *affinity groups*, build *coalitions*, make communication nets (perhaps involving *independent media*) between all members, enjoy your own p*rivate parties*, and solve the problems that you care about, in your own *think tank.*

Affinity groups are groups of people getting together because they share interests. If that sounds like a regular club, give yourself a cigar as a prize (or a candy bar, if you don't smoke.) Define the common areas (Affinities), and you define the group. List your interests, and then start looking. (This one can also give you a checklist. If a group doesn't match up with your checklist, just leave.) Go online and lurk around websites about your hobbies or your interests. Find people you click with and start up some email chains. Look for people who don't play radical games, and talk to them. (Earlier, I talked about some 'trouble' words, to avoid hanging out with rainclouds.) When you've found your set number of people, think about what kinds of rules you want to work by. Most groups use a form of this process. You just want to be aware of the steps while you run through this process. A fun and easy-to-learn game which teaches that process is named "Nomic." This game is about creating and modifying rules for group actions and behavior. (It's also free, which helps the wallet...) Spend a few weekends playing both games. Then go write rules for your group.

Coalition building is all about making connections between two or more groups. Coalition building is matching up the common goals and agendas of different groups into a set of workable relationships. If we want to avoid being, or becoming, or getting invaded by, rainclouds, then we want more sets of eyes. Adding different rational perspectives avoids Group Think – where groups slide into conformity so much that group members stop error checking their activities. Avoiding Group Think needs different thinking styles, as opposed to different appearances/"identities." This is where artificial social situations – Role Playing Games – can come in handy. If your own group needs people that meet certain functions, go write up the needed functions into a set of roles for a Role Playing Game. Then go find people that fit.

STEPS TO BUILDING COALITION

A few basic steps for moving from an Affinity group to a larger coalition:

1.) State the purpose of the new group explicitly – remember to keep it legal.

2.) State what the smaller Affinity groups can provide to the larger coalition.

3.) State what kind of structure (governing/power/etc) the new coalition will have.

4.) State the rules for new affinity groups and/or individuals joining the coalition.

5.) Simulate each of these steps. Rewrite things when needed

6.) Simulate disruptions (Pop Quiz, Hotshot: a mob of rainclouds has shown up at your group's

doorstep. What do you do?) Write up the useful (and legal) procedures.

7.) Give copies of the new rules to each member.

A classic on building and running organizaitons is *Robert's Rules of Order,* by Henry Robert. It has a section on crafting "societies" from scratch. The *Rules of Order* provide a step by step set of instructions to create a full social organization.

The rest of *Robert's* was developed to conduct drama free business sessions. The 7 step list above is a good quick and dirty duct tape style guide to group creation. The *Rules of Order* are for groups that want to connect with the background culture (Going to a city office to obtain a permit? Calling yourself "the chief rememberer" will likely raise some eyebrows. Signing the permit application as "acting secretary and records holder" will likely not raise those eyebrows. Another great point for the more official version is that his rules have stood the test of time. The *Rules of Order* show how to deal with disruptions of groups. Use the proven tricks that will outlast the rainclouds.

The *independent media* culture is growing again, and this scares the snot of the the "traditional media cultures." Not too long ago, there were only a very few publishers that gave some people the opportunity to get their stuff published. If you wanted to get your words out there, you either wrote stuff that agreed with the publisher, or you had to shell out a lot of money to self publish. Now, E-books are very easy to publish. There is no back stock, no lay-out, and no chance of a fire wiping out your work. Print on demand requires just fronting the money for the final formatting of a paper based book and a printing fee. That means it is very hard for the wanna be gatekeepers to put a chokehold on books they don't like. Not too long ago, Being on TV was a very big deal. There were only three main TV networks, and a bunch of smaller stations. Getting on TV meant that you had to have a lot of money, be connected to the people owning the station, or had some sort of information that the TV owners wanted other people to hear. Now, making videos that other people can watch is as easy (and as crude) as swiping the RECORD tab on a smart phone, and then pressing SEND. Find a free text-based web provider and you are on the same floor as any of the old citizen journalists. Get enough people to give you money (legally) and you are a pro. It's pretty obvious that a bunch of reporters in mainstream media are echoing each other, without checking sources. Go out and find or create your own sources of news. If you don't trust MSNBC or Fox, get a group of friends together, build up a list of what you find important, and then report on it.

Creating *private parties* is where things get interesting. Putting money aside for a moment, what stops you from renting a room, deciding on a set of hours for a quiet get-together, and then just lay in a supply of munchies? Got the room at home for folks to come over? What stops you from only inviting those people that YOU like? There's no reason that a private party must be open to the public, or even the rest of a community (house rules and laws always apply, of course.) Put out a spread of food and drinks, and have at it. If you can, build up a rotating list of parties with different communities or groups – a well planned party can strengthen coalitions. Add a set of ice breakers, maybe plan on one room marked for "heavy discussions," and have the rest of the area set aside for low volume music and social conversation. Start with a formal meeting of the groups, go through a quick planned meeting, and then get to the food and drinks. Parties are (usually) fun, and they provide cover for the next option: *think tanks*.

Why should rainclouds have all the fun playing "more erudite than thou." Build your own *think tank* staffed with interesting people showing meshing skills. Planning a think tank gets you more organized about a goal or problem. While putting together a group to bounce ideas around can recharge your batteries, there are a few differences between an informal think tank, and just having a party. Smaller scale think tanks need one seed rule to work out: They need to be focused on solving a problem. All parts and levels/shades/factions are part of a system to solve problems. Design your think tank like a machine to focus on solving that problem. The members need to be picked with an eye for working together to solve that problem. The shared pieces (room, reading materials, simulated whatevers, tools, etc) should boost that focus. (If you want to research energy solutions, a book about basic electricity would boost your focus. Reading about local customer power and energy uses would boost that focus.) Think tanks can avoid burnout by setting time limits. When the problem is solved, the group is done. This is a sticky point, where group loyalty could slow down a solution – so plan a party! Or, counter that by building a Saturday poker game format for creating and running your own group. Every fourth week, the poker group meets with sharable files, paper, pencils, and what all, to figure out solutions to problems. Order take out, close the doors, and set the timers. A longer running version could include plans to study up before future meetings. A smart planner might want to build a cool-down activity, so that think tank members can make a transition back into "normal" social groups.

A few well planned think tanks sharing information can develop a system that "learns" from changing situations - a think tank style party in Dallas might have notes on how one group of cry bullies managed to shut down a meeting. If a think tank in Pittsburgh can get a copy of the Dallas group's notes, then maybe Pittsburgh can spot the warning signs ahead of the game. This is why we should stick to facts and logic, and warn the others - sticking to the facts can help avoid lawsuits, and warning the others builds community.